LIMITS

KEVIN FLEGLER

ASPIRE
PUBLISHING HUB LLC.

Scripture taken from the New King James
Version. Copyright 1982 by Thomas Nelson,
Inc. Used by permission. All rights reserved.

ISBN
978-1-958692-72-1 (Paperback)
978-1-958692-73-8 (eBook)

LIMITS

TABLE OF CONTENTS

Preface

Hidden within each individual is a treasure—a treasure of gifts, talents, and potential. But a treasure hidden beneath the feet doesn't do any good unless one, you know it is there, and two, you are willing to dig it up.

Our culture has seemed to slip away from the concept of the worth, value, and unique greatness of each individual. The value of work and the joy at being productive and skilled in a field doesn't seem to be emphasized as it once was. Excuses for why we aren't successful or why we need assistance seem to abound. And we have a philosophy that government should be right there to provide everything we need.

The philosophy that it is the government's or someone else's job to take care of us acts as a blinder to the truth of the capability and treasure within each person and takes away the incentive to bring it to the surface and develop it. This encouraged slothfulness has allowed rot and decay to begin its creep upon our culture.

There is vast potential for the growth and productivity of our nation. It lies hidden within each individual. Limiting government to its biblical and intended role allows the treasure to be revealed. Discovering and unlocking that treasure will bring great joy and blessings to each person along with a strong nation. My hope is for every person to know the joy, strength, and freedom that comes from being a self-reliant individual, living under a limited government.

THE NEED FOR GOVERNMENT

I suppose that we all tend to think of the times in which we live as being harder, more difficult, or encompassed with more perplexing problems than other times in history. And although the time in which we exist is unique, the core problem we deal with is not; that is, attempting to live in and construct a peaceful society in which our needs are met. Outward circumstances may change. The tools we use to meet our needs may change. But the struggle to live, and live in peace, does not change. A wise man once asked, "Is there anything of which it may be said, 'See, this is new'?"[1] His answer was no in the context of the struggles each generation faces.

Certainly, there are issues within our nation today that are serious problems. The country is divided politically. Unemployment is a real threat to many in society in terms of having their basic needs met. Some fail to see optimism in the future. Our national debt threatens to unravel our entire economic system. The moral foundations that once provided a framework for building character are eroded. I will not say things are worse than they have ever been in our nation's history; I haven't experienced history to make that judgment. These are simply our struggles, our difficulties and our problems to solve. This is our time, and our opportunity to fix the things that are broken. I don't believe these problems are insurmountable or new. I do believe they provide an opportunity to change the course that has brought us to this point. Changing course doesn't mean going back to the "good old days"; we only have today and the hope of tomorrow. Changing course means opening a new door of limitless opportunity.

I believe the course that has brought us here is a government that has stepped outside the role government should have in society. Correcting and changing course means understanding what role government should have and limiting it to that place. We can forgive Woodrow Wilson, the Roosevelts, and other early progressives. I believe they felt they were stepping out on a new course that would bring about the peaceful, fulfilled society we all hope for. But today, we have decades of evidence from around the world of the failure of big government collective isms, and the opportunity to pull from history the system of government that gives the best chance for a society that works.

An argument for limited government necessarily implies a need for government. Limited government does not mean the absence of a government or anarchy. Government is a biblical institution, ordained by God as a part of a well-functioning and peaceful society. (The use of the name God in this document refers to the God who identified himself as the God of Abraham, Isaac, and Jacob; the God of the Hebrew Scriptures, revealed in Jesus Christ, God the son.) Limited government simply means a government that stays within the bounds given by God, a government that is limited in scope and power. Even though my opinions about the power and nature of government are derived from the Bible, I believe the empirical evidence from history supports the proposition that a limited government is the most beneficial to society. It allows freedom and innovation to flourish and advances civilization at an unparalleled pace. My hope is that America may again be a nation ruled by a limited government, and that the blessings of freedom, innovation, and a productive civilization may once again bless our shores.

When an engineer is asked to critique the design of a structure, he will need to know the purpose or need for the structure. Likewise, a mechanic, when replacing a part, needs to be aware of the function of the part. When we look at the government, we too must understand the role it is to play in society, the purpose it is to fulfill, and the need to have a government in society in order to judge if the government we have is doing its job.

So, why do we need a government? I don't believe we can overstate the importance of the question. The answer we give determines exactly what a government should be. The answer gives a basis for defining the role and scope of government, and the limits that should be placed on it. Government is needed because men are evil. Biblically and historically, no matter how broad the authority of a government, or what role that government assumed, the fundamental function of the government was to restrain and punish evil. (Unless specifically indicated by the context, "men" throughout this work refers to mankind and is not meant to be gender-specific.)

Genesis 9:6 states, "Whoever sheds man's blood, by man his blood shall be shed; for in the image of God He made man." This is believed by many to be the first reference to human government in the Bible. In context, this statement occurs after the destruction of all mankind, except for eight people in the flood. God had destroyed the rest of man for his wickedness. In this verse, God seems to be setting a restraint on the wickedness of man by authorizing the punishment of wrong by human hands. This thought is repeated and explained clearly in the New Testament by the Apostle Paul:

> Let every soul be subject to the governing authorities. For there is no authority except from God, and the authorities that exist are appointed by God. Therefore whoever resists the authority resists the ordinance of God, and those who resist will bring judgment on themselves. For rulers are not a terror to good works, but to evil. Do you want to be unafraid of the authority? Do what is good, and you will have praise from the same. For he is God's minister to you for good. But if you do evil, be afraid; for he does not bear the sword in vain; for he is God's minister, an avenger to execute wrath on him who practices evil.
>
> Romans 13:1–4

These verses are very explicit; government is a God-ordained institution, and it exists to punish evil.

This command to be subject to the "governing authorities" is even more profound in light of the fact it was given under the rule of the brutal Roman Empire. But it is important to understand that Paul is not giving a blanket statement for submission to all that a government commands, for Paul himself was later executed by the same government for his disobedience to it by preaching the gospel of Jesus Christ. So he certainly wasn't one of those who had "praise from the same." And we are told elsewhere in Scripture that "we ought to obey God rather than men" (Acts 5:29). There are times when the law of man contradicts the law of God, and our obedience as Christians belongs to God. Paul is speaking of submission to that legitimate function of government that even the Roman Empire performed: the punishment of evil.

It is interesting that governments, which have themselves been very evil, have recognized the need to punish evil and protect the rights of individuals, albeit not all individuals have always been viewed as having rights. Why is there a recognition of evil? What constitutes evil? Where did the concept of rights come from? The debate about the definition of evil and what constitutes a right continues today. But in general, the debate is not about the existence of evil or rights. C.S. Lewis was so perplexed by the awareness in man of right and wrong that it was a key factor in his conversion to Christianity.[2] Without going too deep into a discussion of this awareness, our natural consciousness of evil is a strong argument for a moral lawgiver: our Creator.

As early as 2400 to 2300 BCE, Sargon established an Akkadian nation with laws that recognized the rights of individuals, allowed the poor to have access to the court, and protected the transportation routes to allow commerce to prosper.[3] The Code of Hammurabi dated around 1780 to 1750 BCE is one of the oldest records we have of written law. 282 laws are inscribed on a stone pillar. Interestingly, it gives punishment for theft, injury to others, and murder. It speaks of property rights and the rights of individuals, women, children, and slaves.[4] Recognize the theme? Government exists for the punishment of evil and protection of personal rights.

So if government is needed because men are evil, and there is a biblical and historical precedent that proves that punishment of evil has been a function of government throughout history, how does that help us to determine what government should be like today? Before we answer that, we need to look a little further at the statement that men are evil and broaden our view to the discussion of human nature.

HUMAN NATURE

Humans are unique among God's creation. Not just unique as an evolutionist might look at humans perhaps as an animal that has evolved to a higher intelligence, but unique in that man is a spiritual being. A simplistic way of separating the different parts of creation we are most familiar with would be to speak of the heavens, earth, plants, fish, insects, birds, animals, and man. Man is separate and unique from the other categories. This view is natural to many people. We seem to know we are different from the rest of the world around us. It doesn't take a long study to discover that cultures throughout history have recognized a spiritual component to man. That spiritual component has been expressed in varied ways and by different forms of worship, but it is a common aspect to cultures. So mankind, among God's creation, is a different and unique category. Also, every individual is unique. The very word, *individual*, implies something that is one of a kind. But there are characteristics that are common to all of us as well.

These common characteristics are what I believe can be viewed as our human nature.

Maybe some are disturbed by the statement that men are evil. So what do I mean by that statement? Let's first look at the answer to that from the biblical perspective. I believe the Bible teaches the depravity of man. A simple definition of that is that man is governed by his own interests. We have rejected the sovereignty of God in our lives, and we rule our lives as we choose. This self-interest can lead us to ignore the interests of others, thereby causing harm and injury to others and trampling on and taking away their rights. (We will discuss rights further.) Man, left to his self, is incapable of living in a loving and peaceful society with his fellow man. Peace throughout history has always been short lived and fleeting, something that we pursue but can never quite grasp. To be sure, men have desired it. We have a natural instinct that things should be different, but as a species we are unable to establish a world that lives in peace. Again, it doesn't take a very long look at world history to see that this is the case.

Psalm 14:3 says, "They have all turned aside, they have together become corrupt; there is none who does good, no, not one." The context for this verse is God searching for someone who seeks and knows him. In Romans 3, this psalm is quoted and Paul goes on to write, "For all have sinned and fall short of the glory of God."[1] To "fall short" conveys the idea of missing a target. The meaning is that we have all, fallen short of God's holy standards, and God himself. God is love. Love acts in the best interest of another without regard of the cost to the one loving. We do not measure up to that standard. We love ourselves. Oh, we are capable of loving to a degree. Most parents love and care for their children. We may love a spouse and other family members. Some love their friends. But all people, apart from the work of Christ in them to bring about God's love, have a limit to their love. There is a point where the cost of loving becomes more than we want to give of ourselves. That is a reality of our human nature. That is the basis of evil. It's only a matter of degrees that separate us as men. Some will very quickly elevate themselves and trample other's rights, while some have a greater degree of self-restraint and compassion for their fellow man.

Perhaps before we go on, we should explain the phrase "best interest" as it pertains to love. In some ways it seems superfluous to give an explanation, but in a culture that is at times devoid of biblical values and honestly ignorant of standards of conduct that promote excellence, it may be necessary. "Best interest" refers to those things that will help another to build qualities of honesty, justice, hard work, respect for others, and self-discipline, traits that make a person a productive member of society. It also refers to actions that help another learn love, humility, and self-sacrifice. It doesn't mean always giving another what they want. Sometimes, what we want isn't what we need to build the character mentioned. An illustration that many would understand is a team coach. The coach is hard on players, making them go through tough physical workouts, repetitive drills, and memorizing plays. The coach does all this to produce a winning team. His instructions are in the best interest of the goal. If we want another human being to be happy and productive and to come to faith in Jesus Christ, we must look at others and act in a way toward them that will promote these values. "Best interest" also refers to those actions of mercy, charity, and grace that provide for the helpless and defend the weak. When we do these actions without regard to personal cost, we are acting in love toward another person.

Despite our evil nature, most men still retain a conscience, an awareness of right and wrong, a desire for something better. We retain a shadow of what we were created to be: loving, caring creatures in the image of God living at peace with one another and enjoying the world created for us. This shadow, if allowed to flourish, is still a beautiful creation. Men are gifted by God with many and varied talents. I believe God puts within each of us the ability to do specific things. And if we use those talents, they would bring us great joy and fulfillment in life. We have great minds and great curiosity to explore and discover the workings of the world and universe we were placed in. We look at the stars and are awed by the expanse of the universe. We have a desire to go and explore the unknown reaches of space. Technology has also allowed us to look deeper into the microscopic world around us, and we are increasingly amazed at the vastness of this sphere, unseen by our naked eye. Though our minds may be darkened by sin, they still possess a great ability to learn. We are constantly creating better ways to live within our world. All of this is a gift of God, a hunger he has placed within us to discover what he has created for us. Like a parent that makes a grand playhouse for a child, God has created a whole universe for us to discover and gifted us with the ability to find it out. He takes great pleasure in us exercising those gifts, and we have so much to search out! We have barely scratched the surface. But every individual must be free to use the gifts he is given.

I believe in the greatness of each individual! God, the Master Architect, has given to every man talents and gifts that not only bring joy to daily life, but work together in harmony to have a productive society. Every man and woman of every ethnic background is of equal worth and value.[2] Every human life is uniquely given and gifted by God, and therefore, everyone is equal in value before God.[3] It is from this uniqueness and equality of value that we can begin to develop the concept of rights, and from rights begin to define what is evil with regard to our actions toward other men. All people have a right to their life, a right to use their gifts and talents. We have a right to own property and use the resources around us as they pertain to our talents to accomplish our given tasks. We have a right to the reward of our efforts. And we have a right to store and save that reward for sustaining our life in this world. Evil then, in society, is injuring or taking away a life (life doesn't belong to men; all life belongs to God); preventing people from using the talents given to them; or taking away the reward from the use of those talents. Evil is not limited to an individual. A government can and frequently commits these very evils against innocent citizens.

We have looked at two basic pillars of human nature:

- Men are evil in that our love for others has limits; we are self motivated. For some, it is simply failing to act when we should act. For others it goes so far as taking from another what belongs to them: life, liberty, or property.
- Men are unique and gifted. They are given life and an ability to provide for themselves and society.

Let's go back to our original question. How does knowing that the government is needed because men are evil help to know what government should be like? By expanding our statement that men are evil to a discussion of human nature, we can define what evil is and know what needs to be restrained. But we should also know what needs to be allowed. It is very important to understand how human nature fits into our discussion of government systems. All governments attempt to control and order society and human behavior. In order to control something, you have to know the characteristics of what is being controlled. The characteristics of humans define human nature. The debate about different forms of government has at its root differing views of human nature. If you believe that man is basically good, is capable of caring for others' best interests, and has an ability to achieve a perfect society, then you will favor collective type governments. I believe it can be demonstrated that that is not a correct view of human nature; human nature is as it is described above, and we need a form of government that works with human nature and not against it. In the ensuing chapters, we will discuss just how government works with human nature.

THE UTOPIAN FAILURE

When Sir Thomas More wrote *Utopia* in 1516, he probably had no idea the title of his work would become a branded word, a word that is better known for the idea of a perfect society than for the title of a book written almost five centuries ago. No doubt he would be pleased at that, but I wonder if he would have the same opinions today had he had the same benefit of looking back at the history of those five centuries. It is interesting that the roots for the word *utopia* come from the Greek and mean "nowhere."[1] That is exactly the case. Utopia does not and has not existed anywhere. Why? Because our human nature makes it impossible. Man is not capable of living with the thought of others as his motivation for action. Man is motivated by self.

That is not to fault More for the vision or desire he had for a better government and society. No, it is quite natural for men to long for something better. We seem to instinctively know things aren't the way they should be.

Both as individuals and as a society, we long for and know things should be different. This longing is the emptiness left by man's sin, and is the result of falling away from what we were created to be. Also, More was living in a time that was full of new hope and optimism for some. Only twenty-four years earlier, the American hemispheres had been discovered again by the European continent. This discovery had awakened the senses of innovation and adventure that reside within man. Parts of Europe were ending the period of time referred to as the "Middle Ages," while others had been entering the Renaissance period. Branded into the minds of men were the images of feudal lords and brutal monarchies where men were literally used as pawns to further the interests of any ruling oligarchy. Larger nations had been taking shape, but they were still ruled by monarchs who at times viewed themselves as the only people having rights. From this emergence sprang a hope for something better. Thomas More was arguing for that something better.

His desire was not new or unique. Along with the hope and desire within man for something different, there is also the promise of something better. When ancient Israel left the land of Egypt, they were promised a land "flowing with milk and honey" (Exodus 3:8). The idea conveyed in that expression is a place of peace and plenty of good things. The specific condition for that peace and plenty was the obedience of the people to God's law given at Mt. Sinai (Exodus 19). And because of the disobedience of the people of Israel, that perfect society was not obtained. But God promised a new covenant not just with the people of Israel but with the entire world—a covenant of a time of peace and plenty. Some prophets described it as a time when "everyone shall sit under his vine and under his fig tree, and no one shall make them afraid" (Micah 4:4). Sitting conveys the idea of rest, and his vine and fig tree convey the idea of success in one's own labor. Isaiah described a time when "the wolf also shall dwell with the lamb, the leopard shall lie down with the young goat, the calf and the young lion and the fatling together; and a little child shall lead them" (Isaiah 11:6). He also wrote, "they shall beat their swords into plowshares, and their spears into pruning hooks; nation shall not lift up sword against nation, neither shall they learn war anymore" (Isaiah 2:4). Daniel gives a very specific prophecy concerning the four great empires that have shaped western civilization, and a final empire that would finally bring about world peace and prosperity. In the book of Daniel, chapter 2, Daniel interprets Nebuchadnezzar's dream of a great image constructed of different materials—gold, silver, brass, and iron—with toes of iron and clay. These materials represent four empires: the Babylonian, Persian, Greek, and Roman. Nebuchadnezzar saw a "stone was cut out without hands, which struck the image on its feet of iron and clay, and broke them in pieces" (Daniel 2:34). This stone represents God's kingdom of peace and prosperity that will never be destroyed. This message is repeated in Daniel chapter seven, and in Daniel chapter eight we are told the identity of the second and third kingdoms. Daniel 8:21 gives a specific prophecy concerning the rise of Alexander the Great, and that his empire would be divided into four kingdoms. None of these kingdoms brought about peace and prosperity, and as we look at their history, we are left looking for a kingdom yet to come to fulfill the desire we have for something better.

So, from the Babylonian Empire, through the Roman Empire, to the fall of Rome, the Dark Ages, and the Middle Ages, man has been searching and longing for a perfect society. Into this period of history arrived Thomas More and his vision of an ideal society, a society into which no one owned any property. Everyone worked for the society as a whole. There was no need for money, as what was needed was provided for out of the common store of goods. And indeed, it sounds like a great place—a place without selfishness and greed, a place where everyone cared about his fellow man. But throughout the five hundred years that has passed since then, such a society has remained elusive. It would be another 260 years after *Utopia* had been written before a revolution in America would set in motion events that would begin to overthrow the rule of the European monarchies.

The nineteenth century saw an increase in the desire for freedom across England and Europe. Some monarchies were overthrown, and others had their power weakened. The industrial revolution, however, brought about a division of people into wealthy property owners and a poorer working class. Into this environment came the writings of Karl Marx and Frederick Engels. *The Communist Manifesto*, first published in February 1848, urged the uprising of the working class (proletariat) against the wealthy ruling class (bourgeoisie) and the introduction of a society in which everyone worked for the common good.[2] The stated object of the League of Communists, for which Marx and Engels were asked to write the manifesto, was "the overthrow of the bourgeoisie, the rule of the proletariat, the ending of the old society which rests on class contradiction and the establishment of a new society without class or private property."[3] Unlike Thomas Moore's work that paints a vision of a happy, peaceful place; the work of Marx and Engels seems very dark and foreboding. As I read the *Manifesto*, three words seem to characterize the content: greed, anger, and envy. The image that comes to mind is of men wanting what doesn't belong to them, and angry because they don't have it. This isn't surprising. As atheists, they had rejected a belief in God and were dependent upon themselves as men and a society ruled by men. No longer was there a God in their life who loved them and would meet their needs, a God who had instructed them to be content with what he provided. Now they were left to their own devices, and left lacking, they wanted what other men had. The human nature within them, promoting their own self-interest and preservation, wanted the production of other men. They desired a system of government that would take from those who possessed wealth and distribute it amongst all citizens.

In early November 1917, the communists, under Nikoli Lennon, began to take over Russia and left a record for us to examine of the ability of a communist system to provide a peaceful and beneficial society. The seventy-year history of the Soviet Union and continued communist regimes today leave an abysmal record of poverty and human rights abuses. After seventy years of existence, the Soviet Union collapsed into a bankrupt nation. The twentieth century as a whole is a very sad chapter in humanity. Far from showing the growth in the ability of man to live in peace, it was a century of destruction at an unprecedented level. Not that man has grown worse; other centuries would have been just as destructive if they had possessed the technology we do today. But the twentieth century shows that man hasn't changed. Our basic nature of evil and self-interest is still the same. Let's examine a brief list of some of the deaths brought about by war and political oppression in the last century.

- World War I   13,000,000 to 15,000,000[4]
- Russian Civil War 1918–1922   12,500,000[5]
- World War II   65,000,000 to 75,000,000[6]
- USSR   35,000,000[7]
- Chinese Civil War 1946–1950 6,200,000[8]
- China's "Cultural Revolution" 2,500,000[9]
- Pol Pot   1,770,000[10]
- Vietnam 1960–1975   2,358,000[11]

We could go on and on, but the numbers seem to lose their significance. It's hard for us to grasp that if we were counting to a million, every number would represent an individual person. Perhaps if we put it in terms of sports arenas, it would have more of an impact on us. How many football stadiums would it take to reach the smallest number above of 1.77 million? If we use a figure of 80,000 that some stadiums can hold, it would take over twenty-two stadiums of people to reach 1.77 million. That is twenty-two stadiums of people intentionally murdered for the power and benefit of an evil regime. A look through lists of human rights abuses quickly reveals that communist regimes are very brutal. Besides the brutality, poverty under these same regimes is widespread. It wasn't until China relaxed rules regarding private ownership of property that China's standard of living and wealth began to improve. So why did a system that set out to safeguard the rights of the working class and bring about a higher standard of living for all bring about poverty and brutality instead? Human nature. People are less productive when they don't retain the reward of their efforts. (Our human nature of self-interest and lack of love for others refuses to work as hard for others as we do for ourselves.) And people fail to see that the bourgeoisie (broadly defined as the wealthy ruling class spoken of by Marx and Engels) can never be replaced. The faces in power can change, but because of human nature, the new faces simply become the new wealthy ruling class. The old saying is so true: "Power corrupts, and absolute power corrupts absolutely."[12] It really doesn't matter how political leaders come to power or what system of government they are in; whenever power becomes centralized, abuses will follow. Government power must be limited to act as a barrier to the abuse of power by men.

A recent case in point is the rule of Hugo Chavez in Venezuela. Mr. Chavez was born into a poor family. After spending time in the Venezuelan military, he was involved in a failed coup attempt in 1992. In 1999, he came to power, promising to be a champion for the poor.[13] His villains were the rich oil companies he claimed were stealing the wealth from the people of Venezuela. His socialist regime seized control of the oil industry and later most of the industry within the country. However, the poor still remained poor. Promises were made for the health care and education of the people, but instead of excelling, the people existed at a basic level while Mr. Chavez, his family, and associates amassed billions from the wealth and industry the state had seized.[14] Yet many Venezuelans were content and happy with the crumbs and promises he gave them. The saying "Panem et circenses" still seems to ring true, a sad aspect of another part of our human nature. Men will trade the freedom and opportunity to excel and use the gifts God has blessed them with for a little security and entertainment.

The democratic socialist states of Europe are a picture of this as well. While the citizens of these nations enjoy some freedom and protection of human rights, the nations are beset with high unemployment, high cost of living, and staggering national debt. The trade-off for the promise of cradle to grave government care has been a loss of opportunity to unleash the human potential within the citizens of these great and historic countries. Sir Thomas More's vision of utopia is still nowhere to be found.

THE LIMITATIONS
OF GOVERNMENT

When speaking of the limitations of government at this point, we are not addressing the limits that should be placed on government power, but the limits of what we can expect a government to accomplish. There are limits of what we should expect a government to do, but there are also limits to what any government can do. What are the limiting factors, and what do many people expect?

We will answer the latter first. If we go back to our discussion of Karl Marx and Frederick Engels, we stated that as atheists, they had cut themselves off from the love and provision of God. They had chosen to take the mantle of care upon themselves, and this accounts for the anger, greed, and envy that seems to emanate from their writing. If you have ever struggled swimming, thoughts and desires seem to pass away except for the desire to breathe and reach a place of safety. In any situation in which we are in danger, the nature of self-preservation within us takes over. People will trample over others to get out of a place of danger.

This is the self-interest of our human nature. It explains the insecurity we have about life.

Jesus instructed his followers:

> Therefore do not worry, saying, 'What shall we eat?' or 'What shall we drink?' or 'What shall we wear?' For after all these things the Gentiles seek. For your heavenly Father knows that you need all these things, but seek first the kingdom of God and His righteousness, and all these things shall be added to you. Therefore do not worry about tomorrow, for tomorrow will worry about its own things. Sufficient for the day is its own trouble.

> Matthew 6:31–34

These verses bring great comfort to believers in Jesus Christ. But where do people without faith turn for the security we all desire and seek as people? Many turn to the government.

Again, we see our human nature conditions in the way we act and react, the things we desire, and the insecurities we have. This isn't new. In John chapters six and seven, Jesus told the masses following him at that time that they were following him because he fed them, and only because he fed them. It is in our nature to seek for the security we need and desire. This again goes back to our discussion of Sir Thomas More's *Utopia*. We know we were created for something better. We want to live in a peaceful society in which our needs are met. We crave that and are seeking for that. We have previously reviewed some of the Old Testament promises of such a peaceful time. The New Testament continues that theme and introduces us to the Prince and King who will rule over that society one day: Jesus Christ. When Peter was preaching in Solomon's Porch, he said, "Repent therefore and be converted, that your sins may be blotted out, so that times of refreshing may come from the presence of the Lord, and that He may send Jesus Christ, who was preached to you before, whom heaven must receive until the times of restoration of all things, which God has spoken by the mouth of all His holy prophets since the world began" (Acts 3:19–21).

What many people expect from government is the fulfillment of the prophecies of a future time of peace and plenty, even though they aren't aware that is what they are seeking. The desire for that time is right and natural, but seeking it outside of Jesus Christ will never work. This desire explains the push and slide toward more and more socialist programs. We so crave security that we want promises of being fed, housed, clothed, and doctored from the time we are born until we die. Unfortunately, it isn't just atheists and unbelievers who desire this security from government; many Christians have fallen into this trap as well.

The problem lies in the fact that the government is not God. A government can never keep those promises of care. And as we will see later, this is not the role that God intended for the government. Government is limited in that it is a human endeavor. Yes, it is instituted by

God, but it is operated by man. Men do not have the wisdom and foresight to direct society and orchestrate the gifts and talents of individuals. This is the limiting factor of what a government can do. Government cannot create. Government is not a gifted individual that can take the resources around it and be productive. Government, as an entity, lacks the necessary self-interest to make that happen collectively. A government is filled with individuals, some of whom seek their own self-interest and what they can get, which puts them at odds with the interests of the nation. Therefore, governments have only been able to take from some who have and give it to those who have less and are not producing. Because those who have are not allowed to keep what they have produced, they produce less. Now, there is less to take, and those not producing have consumed what was already given. The end result is the descent of the nation as a whole into poverty. This explains the collapse of regimes and empires that start down the path of being the great provider. Even democratic socialist governments will eventually collapse under the weight of debt. Unable to take enough wealth to sustain the needs for the promises it has given, money is printed or borrowed. When that can't be done any longer, the promises and pledges are changed. People receive less provision, and health care and services begin to be rationed. We already see this in our own nation with the social security program. The benefit age is being raised, and because of a lack of funds, it will continue to be raised until the program is no benefit to anyone. Social Security as it is now will end, either in a way that will provide private ownership and greater opportunity for people to grow their wealth and provide an income in the latter years, or by a descent into declining benefits and bankruptcy.

Government is also limited by the reality of the world in which we live. I remember an episode from the TV series *M*A*S*H** in which Colonel Potter is speaking to Hawkeye who is depressed over the death of a soldier whose life he was trying to save. Colonel Potter gives a succinct lesson in life to Hawkeye by saying, "In war, rule number one is young men die. Rule number two is doctors can't change rule number one." In life, there is the reality of unwanted things, and governments cannot change that reality. There are natural disasters, economic ups and downs, irresponsible people, evil men, sickness, and death. The character of a society is made up of the people who occupy it. A society that looks to the government for all its needs and provisions will only be disappointed by the response the government has to the unwanted things. There were two disasters when Katrina slammed into New Orleans: the disaster and destruction left by the hurricane, and the disaster of a people so dependent on the government to take care of them that many couldn't even be responsible enough to make provisions for their own escape.

Government is limited by what it can do. And when government steps out into areas beyond its responsibility, it will always fail those it has made dependent upon it.

FREEDOM

Freedom is a difficult thing to define. A quick glance at a dictionary on my shelf revealed eleven different definitions of the word. Some that may be familiar are "possession of civil rights; immunity from the arbitrary exercise of authority"; "liberty of the person from slavery, oppression, or incarceration"; and "the right of enjoying all of the privileges of membership or citizenship."[1] In my library, I have a reproduction of Noah Webster's original 1828 dictionary. He lists eight definitions for the word *freedom*. His primary definition is "a state of exemption from the power or control of another; liberty; exemption from slavery, servitude or confinement." A footnote to that states, "Freedom is personal, civil, political, and religious."[2] That last footnote is important. Freedom can be related to those four areas of our life, so the context in which we use the word *freedom* bears great import on the definition that we give.

In our culture today, freedom seems to mean only one thing, which is the primary definition given in my contemporary dictionary: "the condition of being free of restraints."³ Notice the shift toward self-centeredness between Mr. Webster's primary definition in 1828 involving being "controlled by another" to the idea of being "free of restraints." It may seem like a subtle difference until we consider the culture in which these two statements are made. Mr. Webster lived in a society that had struggled and fought for freedom from the tyranny of English rule. I believe that is the control that was fresh in the minds of most Americans of that day. Today, the topic of discussion is frequently freedom from long traditions of right, wrong, and morality. So the idea of being "free from restraints" takes on the meaning of every man doing "what is right in his own eyes."⁴

Perhaps this explains why freedom has become devalued in society and in many parts of the world. Many men fail to grasp the meaning of freedom. It's hard to value or appreciate something that you don't understand or know about. It would probably still be agreed upon today that religious freedom is the choice of conscience to worship as every individual believes or to not worship anything at all. God himself allows every man this freedom of volition as well, as is indicated by his appeal to men to come to him through Jesus Christ. There isn't a compulsion on God's part to bring men to himself, just an appeal for men to look at the evidence and believe. But the greatest meaning of personal, civil, and political freedom has been lost to many. Freedom in that regard is the liberty to use your gifts and talents and the resources around you to provide for your own needs and existence in the world—the freedom to take care of yourself. Personally, it is the freedom to discover your gifts, to develop them, and then to exercise them. Civilly, it is the freedom to use those gifts in your community for your benefit and the benefit of others of your choosing. And politically, it is the freedom to exercise those gifts without the interference or control of the government. The only restriction is that you do not take away that same right and freedom from someone else, in life or in property.

To have that degree of freedom and to use your skills to provide for your own needs bring a great joy and satisfaction to life. A very dear friend introduced me to an expression called "life-work," meaning the thing in life you were born to do. It is that occupation that God has specifically gifted you and equipped you to do. When we are doing that, work no longer becomes labor. It is something we enjoy getting up for and pursuing every day. In part, we have lost that concept because it is not held up as an ideal and taught, the ideal that we are responsible for ourselves. We must provide for our own needs. When the urgency of developing a skill to take care of oneself is gone, we aren't driven to excel. Our human nature that will take the easiest path cheats us of finding out what we are good at doing.

Life is precious to us because we know it ends. A sporting event is exciting because one team will lose. Without consequences for actions, without failure being a real possibility, our actions lose value. In order to know the joy of providing for ourselves, we have to be allowed to fail. We don't naturally like this. The insecurity of our human nature that we have spoken of would rather develop a fail-safe system, a safety net that keeps us from failing. But in doing so, we rob individuals of the chance to excel. We rob people of the opportunity and exhilaration of taking care of themselves. People lose the feeling of self-worth. That is why freedom in this sense is difficult to maintain. People who have lived in a socialist or communist system where security was promised are afraid to give that up and step out on their own. The fear of being independent prevents them from letting go of the meager possessions they are promised. And without this self-reliance being taught, demonstrated, and required by the absence of a government security net, the natural drift (because of our human nature) is toward socialism and government promises.

Self-reliance isn't a bad word. Self-reliance is really God-reliance because it is God who has gifted and designed us with the ability to be productive and meet our own needs. It doesn't matter if a person is a Christian or non-Christian; whenever an individual uses his talents to take care of himself, he is honoring God. Christians especially need to grasp this idea. You are responsible to use the skills God has given you to take care of yourself. No one else has an obligation to feed you if you are an able-bodied individual. God has equipped you, and he expects you to work and provide for your own needs. The admonition in Scripture "If anyone will not work, neither shall he eat"[5] was written to Christians!

Our nation was built on this expression of self-reliance. Whether it was the pilgrims or immigrants coming to a new nation, or settlers expanding west across the prairie, they lived or died by their own efforts. No one promised them success. They were promised opportunity. The land was before them; they could make of it what they willed. By their blood, sweat, sickness, and death, they built a nation, and they experienced an abundant life and freedom! There is no greater boldness, exhilaration, or sense of freedom than to stand and say, "I will live or die by the sweat of my own back and the grace of my God upon me!" Sadly, I believe too few people are familiar with that aspect of life. And too few people have really experienced an abundant life.

My favorite part of Patrick Henry's famous speech before the Second Virginia Convention on March 23, 1775, is not the line with which most are familiar: "Give me liberty or give me death!" Rather, it is his question: "Is life so dear, or peace so sweet, as to be purchased at the price of chains and slavery?"[6] Think about that a minute. Is your life so dear to you, or the perception of peace so precious, that you would trade your freedom for it? Once we experience and know the freedom we've discussed, the answer is as his was: "No!" My life is held in the hands of my God. And by Jesus Christ, though this body will die, I will stand again upon the earth. I will not trade my freedom for a temporary life that I cannot hold on to anyway.

Freedom is feared. As we have seen, some fear the responsibility of freedom. The cost of freedom that each individual must bear is the responsibility to take care of oneself. Our human nature would much rather be cared for. Those in power fear freedom because a free man cannot be easily controlled. When a person loves liberty more than life, it is difficult to find leverage to control such a person. For these reasons, freedom has been something few men have experienced in the context of the history and humanity of the world. And it is in danger of slipping out of the grasp of America.

THE FOUNDER'S VISION

America has never been a utopia. It will never be a utopia. America was not founded as a perfect nation. It was not founded by perfect men. Many times when the word *founders* is mentioned, there will be someone who hears it that gives a roll of the eyes. I don't think the animosity is directed at the men as much as at the ideals of some of the founders that many do not like. I often wonder how many people have ever read letters or documents that were written by the men who founded our nation. Many were brilliant men who had studied history and truly wanted to establish a government that contributed to a peaceful society with happy citizens. *The Federalist Papers* were a series of papers published in New York newspapers for the purpose of persuading the state of New York to support the new constitution. The first striking thing to me about the papers is that they were intended for the average person purchasing a newspaper in New York to read, understand, and be persuaded by. That fact is a powerful statement to the literacy of the American people at that time! The papers are certainly not for easy reading. Yet they weren't written for an elite group of scholars to sit around and debate. It was expected that average citizens would be able to follow the arguments presented. Yet these same men have their writings dismissed and maligned today without the courtesy of a cordial hearing of their work.

To cite one example of these preconceived ideas of disgust, let's examine the issue of slavery. Often, this issue is brought up as an illustration of the warped and flawed view of equality some of the founders had. Slavery and the slave trade were a barbaric and horrific practice that disrespected the rights of the individual and devalued and demeaned the dignity and sanctity of human life. It is and was wrong. The issue, however, provides an illustration of the true value of the founder's contribution to our nation—the vision they had for something better. The value of their work doesn't exist in the totality of the practices established at the time, but in the ideals set forward and the path to equality set before a free people.

It may surprise some that the issue of slavery was debated and discussed at the time the constitution was written. In order to facilitate the passage of the constitution, a provision was inserted in Article V regarding amending the constitution, that no amendment could change the first and fourth clause of the ninth section of Article I before the year 1808. The clauses dealt with the migration and importation of persons and a tax thereon.[1] It is clear from *The Federalist Papers*, number forty-two, that the pertinent points to our discussion of these clauses centered on the slave trade. James Madison, who is attributed with writing number forty-two, wrote,

> It were doubtless to be wished that the power of prohibiting the importation of slaves, had not been postponed until the year 1808, or rather that it had been suffered to have immediate operation. But it is not difficult to account either for this restriction on the general government, or for the manner in which the whole clause is expressed. It ought to be considered as a great point gained in favor of humanity, that a period of twenty years may terminate forever within these States, a traffic which has so long and so loudly upbraided the barbarism of modern policy: that within that period it will receive a considerable discouragement from the federal Government, and may be totally abolished by a concurrence of the few States which continue the unnatural traffic, in the prohibitory example which has been given by so great a majority of the Union.[2]

He goes on to discuss how some used the fact that it would be twenty years before the trade could be abolished as a point of opposition to the proposed constitution. But his point is that to gain the support of enough states to ratify the constitution, this was a compromise that was a step forward in the recognition of the equality of humanity and the end of a barbaric practice. Unfortunately, it took more than twenty years to bring about the result he envisioned. But the vision and a path were set forward.

Another important point is that truth is not made true by the person who speaks it, but it is true because it *is* true. Or another way to put it is: it is true because it agrees with what really is. It is not the purpose of this work to discuss the nature of truth, but it is important to understand that people can speak the truth without practicing it completely in their lives. Many things written by the founders were true, and the failings of some as men doesn't disqualify the ideals and system of limited government that they established.

The reality of our human nature is that it is difficult to change socially accepted practices. Slavery had been an institution in the world for all of recorded history. When the people of Israel came out of Egypt and were given the laws by which they were to be governed, slavery was not abolished, but slaves were given rights and protections from abuse (Exodus 21:1–11, 26–27). Later in Jeremiah 31:31–34, God promised a new covenant in which he would "put my law in their minds, and write it on their hearts." With the coming of Jesus Christ, God revealed to us the equality of all mankind. Galatians 3:27–28 says, "For as many of you as were baptized into Christ have put on Christ. There is neither Jew nor Greek, there is neither slave nor free, there is neither male nor female; for you are all one in Christ Jesus." This ideal of the equality, value, and worth of all mankind became in the days of the founding of our nation more than a theory or idea, but something that would be attempted to be implemented.

Before we go on in our discussion of the founders' vision, it is important to understand that our human nature is still the same today. It is still difficult to change practices that are socially acceptable. I've often wondered how the nation of Germany could have accepted the Nazis' regime and tolerated the genocide of the Jewish people. There are factors of the history of the nation, accepted values, and economic circumstances that can be considered. But for our discussion, human nature again comes into play. The Third Reich went to great lengths at the beginning of the war to make sure the German people weren't inconvenienced by the war. As late as 1943, 1.4 million women were still employed as "household help" in Germany[3] instead of working in armament factories, and every effort was made to maintain the war effort without measures that would "upset the populace."[4] So again, in the self-interest of a majority of people, their needs were being met, and it was socially acceptable to go along with the Nazis' doctrine; to go against it and to stand up for what was right would have incurred personal loss and harm. Love for fellow man had reached a limit that wouldn't be crossed for the majority of the German people.

Our nation today faces a similar moral crisis in denying to a class of citizens the rights and privileges of being a human being with equal worth and value as every other citizen. That is the class of citizens that are alive but unborn. Too many people are caught up in their day-to-day lives and don't give abortion much thought. But as a society, we are denying a basic human right to the most helpless—the right to life. Just as with slavery, intellectuals try to change the definition of what a life is to justify the taking of life. But common sense tells even a small child that there is a little brother or sister growing in mommy's tummy. To any who have been hurt or suffered from the guilt and sadness of abortion, please know there is forgiveness, love, and peace to be found in Jesus Christ.

The vision of the founders is expressed in both of our two important founding documents: the Declaration of Independence and the Constitution. The preamble to the Constitution reads as follows:

> WE THE PEOPLE of the United States, in order to form a more perfect Union, establish Justice, insure domestic Tranquility, provide for the common Defense, promote the general Welfare, and secure the Blessings of Liberty to ourselves and our posterity, do ordain and establish this CONSTITUTION for the United States of America.[5]

This is the purpose for which our constitution was written and adopted—to live in a peaceful society in which our needs are met, the very statement we began our discussion with. This constitution isn't a document to aggrandize certain individuals, but a document that it was hoped would bring the good things listed (Union, Justice, Tranquility, Defense, Welfare, and Liberty) to all citizens. This is the founder's vision. A gift they wanted to give to the posterity of all men and not a select few, which had been the custom of monarchies and empires throughout history. To achieve that, government had to be limited, and citizens needed to rise up and use their God-given talents to provide for their needs and enrich society. This freedom, value, and equality of each individual are expressed succinctly in the Declaration of Independence.

> We hold these truths to be self-evident,
> that all men are created equal, that
> they are endowed by their Creator with
> certain unalienable Rights, that among
> these are Life, Liberty and the pursuit of
> Happiness. That to secure these rights,
> Governments are instituted among
> Men, deriving their just powers from the
> consent of the governed.[6]

I believe, these are the greatest words ever conceived and written by men that weren't inspired directly by God. They represent the culmination of all that can be understood from history and learned from who we are as individuals before God—that we are given life by God, that we ought to be free before God to do his will and use the gifts he has given us for our own happiness and the happiness of society, and that we are accountable only to him for how we decide to use the talents and resources he provides us with. That is liberty and freedom! The next statement in that declaration is equally impressive: that the whole purpose of government is to secure these rights. To secure means to defend and safeguard from evil those rights so that they might not be taken away, to defend those rights from individual men within the nation, and foreign nations without. And that power to secure these rights is granted by the people who possess them. Government of itself has no rights or power. It is ceded to it by the people governed: Hence the phrase in the preamble, "WE THE PEOPLE." That is the founder's vision.

In June of 1850, Frederic Bastiat—a French economist, statesman, and contemporary of Marx and Engels—wrote *The Law*, which presented a stark contrast to *The Communist Manifesto*. Whereas *The Communist Manifesto* is full of anger, envy, and a belief in the state, *The Law* is full of hope, optimism, and a belief in mankind. It is a wonderful discussion of the value and rights of the individual and the potential within man waiting to be released in an environment of liberty versus the control and injustices of socialism. Bastiat expressed the themes of "life, liberty, and the pursuit of happiness" in terms of "life, faculties and production,"[7] life representing our life given and owned by God; faculties being those gifts and talents God has invested us with; and production being the use of those talents and the things those talents produce. Bastiat believed this is what we are as men. These things being given by God are thus owned by him and are entrusted to us as individuals for our use and care. Government exists to protect that production and property that it does not own. When government becomes the entity taking the production of man for expenses other than those incurred in protecting the individual's property, government becomes "the invincible weapon of injustice" and men become victims of "lawful plunder."[8] It is a sad state when a dictator, king, or tyrant is plundering the property of his citizens, but it is even sadder when fellow citizens vote and empower government to take wealth and property from their neighbors and give it to themselves. What is the difference between him walking across the street and taking the property of his neighbor, and asking the government to take it for him? Both are theft, but the latter is said to be "legal."

The founders envisioned a government that was limited to defending the rights of men, a nation whose citizens enjoyed the freedom of using what God had given them to create a peaceful and happy society. Somehow along the way, we have lost sight of the value and potential of the individual. Men do not think highly enough of their capability, and society has eagerly looked to the government for empty promises of security that it cannot fulfill.

PRIVATE PROPERTY RIGHTS

Perhaps we should discuss further the concept of private property rights. My perception is that most people would have some agreement with the concept of a right to life (although there may be disagreement on who has that right), and many would agree with a right to decide what to pursue in life (our concept of liberty or faculties that we have discussed). But, I believe that there is an erosion of the right to personal property. As we have seen in the statements of Jefferson and Bastiat, property was included in their list of rights. Jefferson expressed it as "the pursuit of happiness," while Bastiat expressed it as "production." "The pursuit of happiness" relates to the right to own property in the sense that our liberty is useless without the right to use the resources around us to produce those things we need to sustain and enjoy our physical existence in this world. Man is not God. We cannot create something from nothing. We can only fashion and build from the natural resources that God has provided for us. Property rights are essential for motivating man in his fallen evil state to use the gifts given him by God. We will discuss this in more detail later, but we made the statement earlier that government needs to work with human nature and not against it. Property rights are necessary for that. Because man's human nature is based on self-interest, the ability to acquire and maintain property and wealth will motivate man to be productive and produce goods and services that are beneficial and necessary for all society. Doesn't this seem like selfishness? Yes. Is that honoring to God? Selfishness of itself is not a righteous quality, but self-interest as a motivator for man to be productive and responsible for his own needs does honor God, and here is why.

God is our Creator and giver of our life and talents. As such, he owns all mankind. We are accountable to him for how we use the talents he has given us, and self-reliance is really God-reliance because we are depending on what he has given us. Again, this is true and honoring to God whether the individual even believes in God. In the same way, God created the earth and property. What we as men make with these natural resources God wants us to retain, and we should be responsible to him for how we use that property. All men are accountable to God for what they do with their property. It is not in God's design for the government to be the decision-maker for how man's production is used. When government steps in and takes private production and property for purposes other than its legitimate function (the defense of individual and national rights), government is robbing man of his accountability before God for the use of that property.

Private property rights have long been established in the Bible. In the long account of Abraham's life, his property and wealth is spoken of as belonging to him, a blessing from God. Jacob and his sons took their property with them to Egypt. When the children of Israel left Egypt, the Egyptians gave their property—"articles of silver, articles of gold, and clothing"—to the people of Israel (Exodus 12:35–36). In Exodus 20:15, a command is given: "You shall not steal." If stealing is taking what does not belong to you, then it naturally implies the right of an individual to own property. Later in Exodus, punishments are spelled out for stealing or injuring the property of others. The concept of property rights are stated and implied throughout the rest of the Old Testament. Even wicked King Ahab was hesitant to take the vineyard that belonged to Naboth. And Jezebel had to scheme and plot Naboth's death in order to take possession of what didn't belong to them. God commanded Elijah to speak to Ahab, "Have you murdered and also taken possession?" (1 Kings 21).

Property rights are confirmed in the New Testament as well. Jesus spoke frequently of money and how to use it wisely. Jesus spoke of money and wealth as being a test of our faithfulness of God's resources. In Luke 16:10–11, Jesus said, "He who is faithful in what is least is faithful also in much; and he who is unjust in what is least is unjust also in much. Therefore if you have not been faithful in the unrighteous mammon, who will commit to your trust the true riches?" Mammon refers to the world's riches, and it is called unrighteous in comparison to the spiritual riches and blessings of God.

One of my favorite parables that illustrates God's view of property and fairness that is in stark contrast to the view of many people is in Matthew 20:1–15. Though lengthy, it is worth inserting here.

> For the kingdom of heaven is like a landowner who went out early in the morning to hire laborers for his vineyard. Now when he had agreed with the laborers for a denarius a day, he sent them into his vineyard. And he went out about the third hour and saw others standing idle in the marketplace, and said to them, 'You also go into the vineyard, and whatever is right I will give you.' So they went. Again he went out about the sixth and the ninth hour, and did likewise. And about the eleventh hour he went out and found others standing idle, and said to them, 'Why have you been standing here idle all day?' They said to him, 'Because no one hired us.' He said to them, 'You also go into the vineyard, and whatever is right you will receive.' So when evening had come, the owner of the vineyard said to his steward, 'Call the laborers and give them their wages, beginning with the last to the first.' And when those came who were hired about the eleventh hour, they each received a denarius. But when the first came, they supposed that they would

receive more; and they likewise received each a denarius. And when they had received it, they complained against the landowner, saying, 'These last men have worked only one hour, and you made them equal to us who have borne the burden and the heat of the day.' But he answered one of them and said, 'Friend, I am doing you no wrong. Did you not agree with me for a denarius? Take what is yours and go your way. I wish to give to this last man the same as to you. Is it not lawful for me to do what I wish with my own things? Or is your eye evil because I am good?'[1]

I love how this whole parable speaks against what socialism and much of our society would call fair and right. But God is showing us what is truly right. The key question for our discussion is, "Is it not lawful for me to do what I wish with my own things?" The landowner is clearly offering the going rate because he is able to hire workers immediately in the morning. He harbors no ill will to any workers when he calls them "friend." All that is called in question is his goodness and generosity for giving even those who only worked one hour a day's wage. He asserts his right to do what he wishes with his property. The only evil revealed in the story is the greed of the workers who wanted what did not belong to them.

Many Christians and churches have the mistaken concept that socialism is a Christian doctrine. This is just not true. God expects the individual to be accountable to him for how he uses the resources God has entrusted him with. We will discuss later that God never intended government to be the instrument of charity. Sometimes the first chapters in the book of Acts are cited as examples of the church being and acting socialist. Again, this is mistaken. It is true the believers in Jerusalem in the early days of the church sold their possessions and gave them to the church to distribute to those in need. And none lacked because of the love of the believers to see that everyone's needs were met. The key point is that this was a *voluntary* action on the part of each believer. Every believer was only accountable to God for how he decided to use his possessions. This is clearly brought out in Acts 5:1–10.

> But a certain man named Ananias, with Sapphira his wife, sold a possession. And he kept back part of the proceeds, his wife also being aware of it, and brought a certain part and laid it at the apostles' feet. But Peter said, 'Ananias, why has Satan filled your heart to lie to the Holy Spirit and keep back part of the price of the land for yourself? *While it remained, was it not our own? And after it was sold, was it not in your own control?* Why have you conceived this thing in your heart? You have not lied to men but to God.' Then Ananias, hearing these words, fell down and breathed his last....Now it was about three hours later when his wife came in,

not knowing what had happened. And Peter answered her, 'Tell me whether you sold the land for so much?' She said, 'Yes, for so much.' Then Peter said to her, 'How is it that you have agreed together to test the Spirit of the Lord?'[2]

The text makes several things clear: Ananias and Sapphira were struck dead for lying, and what they owned was theirs to do with what they willed.

Private and personal property rights are important for two key reasons: all individuals are accountable before God for what they choose to do with their property, and private property rights are the motivation for men to use their gifts and talents to be productive.

FEDERAL EXPANSION

If government is needed because men are evil and infringe on the rights of one another, and government exists "to secure these rights," how has our government stepped outside of those limits? Each of us can probably come up with examples in our lives when we were shocked that there were laws that regulated an activity (of freedom and liberty as we have defined it) that we didn't feel the government had any business regulating. The federal government seems to be everywhere, and it's about to get much worse. With the passage of the Patient Protection and Affordable Care Act of 2010 (Obamacare), the federal government will be involved in every aspect of our life.

For those of us who don't deal with bureaucracy on a regular basis, an apt illustration of what our future holds is a visit to your local DMV office. This is actually one of the predominantly legitimate functions of government, both on a state and federal level. Public highways promote freedom, personal as well as commercial. They are accessible for all and do not promote or favor one industry over the other. Safe roads and safe vehicles traveling on those roads are reasonable requirements and would fall under the category of government defending our right to life and promoting our liberty to transport the goods produced by our talents. However most visits to a DMV office to fulfill our obligations for the vehicles we wish to use on public roadways are frustrating. Long lines, confusing rules, and an endless stack of papers that must be filled out just right, on the right form, to receive any service. After waiting in line, if you have the incorrect form, it's a formal request for the correct one, a wait at the mail box, and back in line. Replace the DMV in our illustration with your local health care facility, and that is what awaits us with government-run health care.

It's completely irrational how anyone could infer from our constitution that the federal government has any power to compel us to buy any product (health insurance), or that they have any power to be involved in our private health care choices and decisions. Yet the Supreme Court (*National Federation of Independent Business v. Sebelius, Secretary of Health and Human Services, 2011*) has upheld just such a power. Though not upholding the law through the Commerce Clause (which we will discuss further), a majority of the court found that the mandate to buy insurance was constitutional under the power of Congress to tax. It's quite a talent to take words requiring people to buy a product and declare them to mean a new tax. And a look at the opinion reveals it took a lot of words to try and explain how to get from buying to taxing.

Part of the blame lies with a culture that is growing ever more accepting and desirous of government entitlement programs. In 2012, 62 percent of the federal budget went to entitlement programs that include Medicare, Medicaid, Social Security, and welfare programs.[1] An entitlement is a "right" to financial benefits given by the government to those who qualify for certain programs. Entitlements given to businesses are generally called subsidies. Social Security, while promoted in the 1930s as a retirement program, has simply become another entitlement. Current retirees are paid with the taxes of current workers. The money that was taken from former wage earners was spent by Congress long ago. Entitlements and subsidies are destructive to the economy and productivity. They are destructive to the economy because they take money out of the hands of those who produce and put it where it will just be consumed. Personal entitlement dollars aren't reinvested by individuals to produce goods or services, but they are potential investment dollars taken from workers and business taxpayers, thereby reducing capital for economic expansion and growth. They destroy productivity by destroying incentive to work and save on an individual basis, and to be innovative and competitive (or even profitable) at a business level. Both rob individuals of the opportunity and incentive to use their gifts and talents and thus experience the joy and freedom of excelling!

As we have already stated, these programs are not sustainable. The unfunded mandates of current entitlements (promises the government has already made to make a future payment) are approaching \$86,800,000,000,000 (that's trillion!).[2] There simply isn't enough money to keep those obligations. No matter who promises to save these programs, it won't happen. They are finished as they exist now. Either people must be allowed to exit the programs and take care of themselves while providing for current retirees (in the case of Social Security), or the programs will be rationed out of existence by increasing the requirements for benefits (raising the retirement age to the point very few receive any payments; that is, you die first).

Another reason we have reached this level of expansion in the powers of the federal government is the fact politics has become professionalized. This aspect of government feeds on itself. The more services the government can offer, the more work created, and the more reasons politicians find to stay in Washington. I chuckle when I read Article I, Section 4, Clause 2 of the Constitution. It reads, "The congress shall assemble at least once in every year, and such meeting shall be on the first Monday of December, unless they shall by law appoint a different day."[3] The framers envisioned a federal government so limited in the breadth of power that there wouldn't be much to do, deeming it necessary to insert the above language. The decisions, issues, and debate about the role of government in the individual's life would be left to the states to decide. These issues were deemed outside the role of the federal government. This would lend itself to a citizen legislature, where the bulk of the legislators' time was spent being a productive member of society instead of an elite ruling class. This doesn't mean all politicians have fallen into this category. There are many individuals in the House and the Senate who truly care about our nation and want to fix our problems, but too many only care about their position and power.

This elitism seems to have spilled over into the Supreme Court as well. The Constitution is a simple document. The primary role of the Court has been to review the constitutionality of federal laws (*Marbury v. Madison, 1803*), constitutionality of actions by a state (as an entity), and since the Fourteenth Amendment, constitutionality of state law as it relates to an individual and their rights as a United States citizen. Given some of the decisions that have come from the court, I would much rather have citizens of respected character who have been successful in their career and endeavors of life be appointed to the Court and give judgment based on a common reading of the Constitution than some of the lawyers and academics that are currently seated.

It is amusing and baffling the debate that can be generated when people abandon basic principles of reading and interpretation. Besides the above mentioned case concerning the Affordable Care Act, the Second Amendment provides a case in point. "A well regulated Militia, being necessary to the security of a free State, the right of the people to keep and bear Arms, shall not be infringed."[4] That is the Second Amendment—one simple sentence. The militia was defined in 1828 as

> the body of soldiers in a state enrolled for discipline, but not engaged in actual service except in emergencies; as distinguished from regular troops, whose sole occupation is war or military service. The militia of a country are the able bodied men organized into companies,

regiments and brigades, with officers of all grades, and required by law to attend military exercises on certain days only, but at other times left to pursue their usual occupations.[5]

The term *militia* in the amendment defines the type of arms being referred to as those carried by the common soldier. The only difference between the militia and regular troops is the term of service. The phrase "the people" refers to the citizens of the nation. Thus, this one sentence amendment practically means that all citizens have a right to keep and carry any arm that is common to that carried by the average infantryman, as all lawful citizens are responsible for the defense of their state and nation. That makes some people uncomfortable, which is fine. If people are opposed to the amendment, they can start an effort to have it repealed or changed to, "Hunting being an American tradition, the right of the people to own a shotgun shall not be infringed." But don't try and change the meaning of the amendment as it is now. When words lose their meaning, everything loses meaning, and we find ourselves in a culture without any meaning or values.

To further examine the expansion of the federal government's powers, we will look at three specific areas that I believe have allowed the federal government to have, at this point, unlimited power. They are the abuse of the Commerce Clause, the abandonment of federalism, and the income tax.

FEDERAL EXPANSION: THE COMMERCE CLAUSE

What is known as the "Commerce Clause" is found in Article I, Section 8, Clause 3, of the Constitution. In listing the powers of Congress, this clause states, "To regulate Commerce with foreign Nations, and among the several States, and with the Indian Tribes."[1] The phrase "among the several States" is where the idea of Congress regulating interstate commerce comes from. The concept of Congress regulating interstate commerce has been defined so broadly by the courts over the years that it is difficult to engage in an activity that wouldn't be considered interstate commerce. The original thought behind the phrase and the need for its inclusion in the Constitution as a delegated power was to ensure the free flow of goods and services between the states, basically to insure a robust, free market and cooperation between the states.

There is one great overriding premise by which the federal Constitution—every article, section, clause and amendment—needs to be interpreted. That is, the Constitution was designed and intended to give the absolute minimum powers necessary to the federal government for it to be still considered a government. Under the Articles of Confederation, for most purposes the individual states were acting like separate and sovereign nations. The national government as it existed then lacked power over individual citizens as members of one nation. Power was basically limited to that over the states collectively with no practical means of enforcement for actions contrary to the Articles. The deterioration of a national identity and unity within and a respected governing authority for foreign nations to deal with America as a whole led to the convention to amend the Articles of Confederation in May of 1787, from which the Constitution was drafted. The individual states were rightfully (as we will see in our discussion of federalism) reluctant to cede power to a national government. Thus, the Constitution was intended, drafted, and explained to be the smallest quantity of delegated powers required for there to be a United States, with all other powers left to the states. Therefore, interpretation of the Constitution must be limited to this narrow scope of delegated power.

A summary of this is given in *The Federalist*, number 15. The context for the following quote regards the discussion of a league or alliance versus a government.

If the particular States in this country are disposed to stand in a similar relation to each other, and to drop the project of a general DISCRETIONARY SUPERINTENDENCE, the scheme would indeed be pernicious, and would entail upon us all the mischiefs that have been enumerated under the first head: but it would have the merit of being at least consistent and practicable. Abandoning all views toward a confederate Government, this would bring us to a simple alliance offensive and defensive; and would place us in a situation to be alternatively friends and enemies of each other as our mutual jealousies and rivalships nourished by the intrigues of foreign nations should prescribe to us.

But if we are unwilling to be placed in this perilous situation; if we will still adhere to the design of a national government, or which is the same thing as a superintending power under the direction of a common Council, we must resolve to incorporate into our plan those ingredients which may be considered as forming the characteristic difference between a league and a government; we must extend the authority of the union to the persons of the citizens, -the only proper objects of government.[2]

The idea that the new federal government would have authority over the "persons of the citizens" of the several states was frightening to many, and the reason for the limited nature of the federal government and inclusion of the Bill of Rights in the Constitution. It is important and essential to have this understanding of the origination of the Constitution to have an understanding of what the Commerce Clause means. We stated earlier that the clause was meant to ensure the free flow of goods and services between the States. In discussing this clause, *The Federalist*, number 42, states,

> I shall confine myself to a cursory review of the remaining powers comprehended under the third description, to wit, to regulate commerce among the several States...The defect in power in the existing confederacy, to regulate the commerce between its several members, is in the number of those which have been clearly pointed out by experience... A very material object of this power was the relief of the States which import and export through other States, from the improper contributions levied on them by the latter. Were these at liberty to regulate the trade between State and State, it must be foreseen that ways would be found out, to load the articles of import and export, during the passage through their jurisdiction, with duties which would fall on the makers of the latter, and the consumers of the former.[3]

In light of the minimum required powers view of the Constitution and the explanation of the clause cited, the Commerce Clause should be limited to extending power to the federal government only as it relates to the free flow of goods and services. Sadly, almost any string that can be found to relate an activity to commerce between state lines has been defined as falling under the power of the Commerce Clause, and Congress has used this clause as an excuse to regulate and intervene in our day-to-day lives.

At times, the Supreme Court has tried to limit the use of this power, but we seem to constantly slip back into a broad definition of the clause. In *Schechter Poultry Corp. v. United States (1935)*, the court struck down a law requiring a minimum wage. Chief Justice Hughes, discussing the power of the federal government to control wages under the authority of the Commerce Clause, wrote that

> it is not in the province of the Court to consider the economic advantages or disadvantages of such a centralized system. It is sufficient to say that the Federal Constitution does not provide for it. Our growth and development have called for wide use of the commerce power of the federal government in this control over the expanded activities of interstate commerce, and in protecting that commerce from burdens, interferences, and conspiracies to restrain and monopolize it. But the authority of the federal government may not be pushed

to such an extreme as to destroy the distinction, which the commerce clause itself established, between commerce "among the several States" and the internal concerns of a State.[4]

In many subsequent cases, the court drifted away from that view, but in 1995 in *United States v. Lopez*, the court again tried to limit Congress's abuse of this clause. The case involved a law banning guns within a thousand feet of a school, which Congress claimed it had authority to do under the Commerce Clause. In a concurring opinion by Justice Clarence Thomas, he wrote,

> Although I join the majority, I write separately to observe that our case law has drifted far from the original understanding of the Commerce Clause. In a future case, we ought to temper our Commerce Clause jurisprudence in a manner that both makes sense of our more recent case law and is more faithful to the original understanding of that Clause.[5]

And regarding the "substantial effect" test, which means that any activity substantially effecting interstate commerce falls within the power of Congress to regulate that activity, Justice Thomas wrote, "This test, if taken to its logical extreme, would give Congress a 'police power' over all aspects of American life. Unfortunately, we have never come to grips with this implication of our substantial effects formula."[6]

The Commerce Clause of the Constitution was meant to provide for free and robust economic activity among the states and was never meant to be used by Congress as a tool to interfere with the free exercise and use of the talents of the people to create that economic activity. The federal government must be limited to an original view of the clause to restore freedom and economic growth.

FEDERAL EXPANSION: THE ABANDONMENT OF FEDERALISM

A federal government is defined as "a form of government in which a union of states recognizes the sovereignty of a central authority while retaining certain residual powers of government."[1] Specifically, as it pertains to our government, our system is best defined by the Tenth Amendment to the Constitution which states, "The powers not delegated to the United States by the Constitution, nor prohibited by it to the States, are reserved to the States respectively, or to the people."[2] We have already gone into some detail about the intention of the framers for a federal government that would be limited to the minimum powers necessary for a central government to exist. In *The Federalist*, number 32, Alexander Hamilton states, "But as the plan of the Convention aims only at a partial union or consolidation, the State Governments would clearly retain all the rights of sovereignty which they before had and were not by that act exclusively delegated to the United States."[3] He went on to enumerate three specific cases in which this would be so: powers granted to the Union, prohibited to the States, or authority that would be "absolutely and totally contradictory and repugnant."[4] Similarly, James Madison wrote in *The Federalist*, number 39, "In this relation then the proposed Government cannot be deemed a national one; since its jurisdiction extends to certain enumerated objects only, and leaves to the several States a residuary and inviolable sovereignty over all other objects."[5]

Although the Supreme Court through the years has maintained a good degree of this intent by the framers, culturally we have drifted from the wisdom and value of a federal system. The benefit of the federal system lies wherein power resides. The closer the seat of power to the people, the more control the people have over their government. It is much easier for a citizen to know, speak to, and have interaction with their state legislature than their federal one simply because of proximity. This puts the power of the government back into the hands of the people. It also maintains local control over local problems. The people residing in a state or smaller locality are the best ones to make decisions for their area while still enjoying the civil rights and protections granted them federally as United States citizens.

It is interesting that even though the courts have maintained the rights of the states to be free from certain interventions by the federal government, the federal government has nonetheless gained a broad power over the states in issues such as entitlements, transportation, and education. How has this happened? Basically, the federal government bribes the states to do what the federal government wants, and the states, failing to stand on principle, have reached out with greedy hands and agreed to the terms demanded of them. Even in the aforementioned case of *National Federation of Independent Business v. Sebelius*, the Supreme Court ruled that the provision in the Affordable Care Act requiring states to expand coverage for Medicaid was unconstitutional because it would take away all funding to the states for Medicaid as punishment for failure to comply, and not just the additional funding promised for expansion.[6] Yet despite this ruling, many of the states that originally brought suit are now lining up to get the promised dollars.

Besides the bent in our culture to seek security and welfare from the government, we began to drift from the federal concept and importance of state sovereignty over all issues not specifically delegated to the federal government years ago. Originally, in Article I, Section 3, Clause 1, of the constitution, senators were to be chosen by the state legislatures. The Senate was supposed to be the body of the states. *The Federalist*, number 39 explains, "The Senate on the other hand will derive its powers from the States, as political and coequal societies."[7] And regarding selection of the senators by the legislature of the respective state, number 62 of *The Federalist* explains,

> It is recommended by the double advantage of favouring a select appointment, and of giving to the state governments such an agency in the formation of the federal government, as must secure the authority

of the former; and may form a convenient
link between the two systems.[8]

The idea was that the legislatures of the states would be more keenly aware of the encroachment of the federal government upon the rights of the state and better able to hold senators accountable for their actions in regard to the state.

Since the enactment of the Seventeenth Amendment in 1913, senators have been chosen by direct election of the people. The benefits of having a legislative body representing the interests of the states have been lost. Freedom is best preserved when individual states retain control over state issues. Greater political power is vested in the hands of the people when the federal government is limited to the powers delegated to it in the Constitution, and the remaining power is left to the states. That is the federal system we need to return to so we can regain freedom and opportunity.

FEDERAL EXPANSION: THE INCOME TAX

Today, the federal government is funded largely by the income tax, but that hasn't always been the case. Before 1913, our national government was funded predominantly through duties, taxes, and excises on imports and items of commerce. In order for a government to perform its legitimate functions, it must have a source of revenue. Two important sections of the Constitution that deal with the method of taxation are both in Article I. Section 2, Clause 3 states, "Representatives and direct taxes shall be apportioned among the several states."[1] Section 9, Clause 4 reads, "No capitation or other direct tax shall be laid, unless in proportion to the census or enumeration herein before directed to be taken."[2] A capitation is another name for a poll tax, or a tax assessed to each individual. That is a type of direct tax. The method used to determine the amount of tax may vary, but a direct tax is assessed to the individual. An example of an indirect tax would be a tax assessed to goods or services. The tax goes with the product, and whoever purchases the product pays the tax. The framers were again emphasizing the federal concept of the equality of the states by making sure no state would pay an unbalanced share of the national government budget through an assessment of direct taxation. All direct taxes would be based on the population of the state just as representation is.

The Federalist Papers deal with the issue of taxation extensively in numbers 30–36. In 36, the point above is emphasized.

> Let it be recollected, that the proportion of these taxes is not to be left to the discretion of the national Legislature; but is to be determined by the numbers of each State as described in the second section of the first article. An actual census or enumeration of the people must furnish the rule; a circumstance which effectually shuts the door to partiality or oppression. The abuse of this power of taxation seems to have been provided against with guarded circumspection. In addition to the precaution just mentioned, there is a provision that 'all duties, imposts, and excises, shall be UNIFORM throughout the United States.[3]

The income tax was first implemented in 1862 in an effort to fund the Union during the Civil War. It was ended in 1872. It was implemented again briefly in 1894 and 1895, but was challenged and ruled unconstitutional because, as a direct tax, it was not proportional among the population of the states.[4] If incomes were higher in one state than another, a state with a lower population could end up paying a larger share of the national budget. In 1913, the Sixteenth Amendment was added to the Constitution. "The Congress shall have power to lay and collect taxes on incomes, from whatever source derived, without apportionment among the several States, and without regard to any census or enumeration."[5] Thus, our modern income tax was born.

The modern income tax was born out of the progressive movement. The progressive movement was reactionary to the growing wealth and power of those who were making fortunes from the industrial revolution. The time period between the middle nineteenth century and early twentieth century marked a change in societies around the world. Many were shifting from an agrarian society to an industrial one. This new phase was unparalleled in many respects. There wasn't a historical model to look at and deal with the new social issues that this shift presented. There were abuses of workers, monopolies, unjust business practices, and a perception of politicians who worked for industry rather than the concerns of constituents. In the United States, the progressive movement was a response to this. The Sixteenth and Seventeenth Amendments were both adopted in 1913 as a part of this movement. As we have discussed, the Seventeenth Amendment changed the election of Senators to a direct election by the people, part of the progressive concept to put power into the people's hand. Antitrust laws and other pushes were made to limit and regulate business. Some of these responses were appropriate. A business, just as an individual or a government, should not take away the basic rights and freedoms of life, liberty, and property we have discussed and defined. But neither do the people have a right to collectively, through the government, take away the rights of legitimate, successful businesses and their owners. In many aspects, the income tax has become a tool to promote class warfare, and a club to punish the wealthy.

It is not a crime or a sin to be wealthy. We have already discussed that all individuals are accountable before God for the use of their talents and resources. There are evil wealthy people and there are evil poor people. We hear of the abuses of some of the wealthy, but we usually do not hear of the generous hearts of many of the wealthy. The founder of the company that bears his name, J.C. Penney, was well known for his generosity. R.G. LeTourneau wanted to build a better way to move dirt, and he did. Nearly three hundred inventions can be attributed to his efforts. His companies were responsible for producing 70 percent of the earth-moving equipment used by the army in WWII. He founded a college, funded missionaries, and set up a foundation that distributed 90 percent of his salary as well.[6] The demonization of the wealthy usually reveals the greed and envy of those who do it. Money is not the root of all evil. "For the love of money is a root of all kinds of evil" (1 Timothy 6:10). To want what someone else has rightfully earned is a covetousness that shows a heart fixed on the love of money.

Besides being viewed as a punitive tool, the income tax dampens production. Going back to our human nature, we are motivated by our own self-interest. A great motivator in that regard is the reward we get for our efforts. The income tax takes away the reward of our efforts. This is a disincentive for us to be as productive as we might be otherwise. This is more of a factor in the decision-making processes we all go through than we might realize. In our careers, we look at what tax bracket we will be in. To barely cross over into a higher bracket usually results in less take-home income than staying in the position we are at. This disincentive to be productive is compounded for businesses, that face a plethora of tax laws. The fact the mortgage interest deduction is so popular shows that people pay attention to the tax ramifications of their actions. A robust economy requires decisions to be made based on the potential reward, not on how the decision will affect our tax liability. Full reward means full production, which benefits everyone in terms of more jobs and an expanded economy. There are no limits to economic potential. When men are free to use their gifts and talents and promised the reward of their efforts, the economy will continually trend upward and expand. The inevitable downturn cycles will be brief, and then the upward trend will continue.

The income tax also allows the government to control economic activity. Our current tax code is extremely complex and burdensome to comply with. That in itself makes it unproductive. "It might be demonstrated that the most productive system of finance will always be the least burdensome" (*The Federalist Papers*, number 35).[7] The reason for the complexity is a constant debate and struggle over what is or isn't considered income, what of that which is considered income will be deductible, and a constant parade of interest groups that want exceptions to the rules. No one likes to see the reward of their efforts taken away, so we are always pleading with Congress to let us keep more of what is ours. If we grasp what power that places in the hands of Congress, we will understand why it is so difficult to have tax reform. Congress can change and control economic activity, and punish whoever they wish by adding or crossing out a line in the tax code. They become the puppeteer and we the marionettes dancing at the end of their string. The reason the Constitution required direct taxes to be proportional was to, "shut the door to partiality or oppression."[8] We have abandoned the proportional directive, and we have in the income tax, partiality and oppression.

No one likes to pay taxes, but they are necessary for the government to fund its legitimate functions. Dollars taken from the economy by the government are fewer dollars in the hands of citizens to produce. Government spending needs to be as small as possible, and it could be dramatically reduced if government were restricted to its delegated powers. A better way to collect the necessary revenue is through the indirect taxation of economic activity rather than reward. The benefit of taxing economic activity (compared to other systems) is eloquently stated in *The Federalist*, number 21.

> Imposts, excises and in general all duties upon articles of consumption may be compared to a fluid, which will in time find its level with the means of paying them. The amount to be contributed by each citizen will in a degree be at his own option, and can be regulated by an attention to his resources... It is a signal advantage of taxes on articles of consumption, that they contain in their own nature a security against excess. They prescribe their own limit; which cannot be exceeded without defeating the end proposed – that is an extension of the revenue.[9]

The reason these taxes find their own level and "prescribe their own limit" is that they are paid by the choice of purchasing a product. If the tax rate for a product is too high, sales will decline and the tax revenue will decrease. If the tax rate is acceptable to the consumer, sales will be based on the economic value of the product. Notice who is in control of the tax rate. Ultimately, it is the consumer and not the Congress. Eliminating the income tax puts power back into the hands of the people.

We have briefly examined three circumstances that have allowed the federal government to step outside the limits originally intended in the Constitution:

1. The abuse of the commerce clause, allowing federal authority into our every day economic activity

2. The abandonment of the federal system through the bribery of the states by the federal government, destroying the authority of the states over state issues

3. The adoption of the income tax, destroying incentive and productivity, and granting control of economic activity to Congress

GOD'S DESIGN
FOR AN ORDERED
SOCIETY

One of the wonderful things about the Bible is that the principles given within it work regardless of the faith of the people following them. When a man and woman follow the principles for marriage given in the Bible, they will have a happy and fulfilled marriage. It doesn't matter if they are Christian or not (though there is a part of us and marriage that can only be filled by Christ); following the principles will bring about a positive result. The reason for this is that God's Word is truth.

We live in a time where many have adopted a postmodern world view, a view in which the idea of an objective truth is questioned and many times mocked. This isn't entirely new. People often become disillusioned with the confusion, hurt, and failure of life. The world is full of advice; people and groups calling out do this, do that, follow this person, all with the promise of happiness and success. When we are young, we often hold to ideals and believe we can change the world. But as we grow older, we see that nothing has changed. The world and people remain the same. That's because man cannot change human nature. Over two thousand years ago, another individual was disillusioned with the reality of life. Perhaps he started out with the ideal of the glory of the Roman Empire. But over time, he realized there wasn't any glory, just people using power for their own aggrandizement at the expense of the lives of others. The Roman Empire couldn't change the human heart. This man, Pontus Pilate, asked the sinless Son of God, the only one who can change our hearts, "What is truth?" (John 18:38).

Even in this book, I am making an appeal, a plea to follow this advice to have a happy and fulfilled society. Why should these words be listened to? Is it just another path that will end in failure? No. Why can I be so assertive? Because the principles laid out are founded upon God's Word, the truth.

Truth agrees with what is. It mirrors reality. We can look at words that claim to be truth, turn and compare them to what we see and experience in the object of those words, and make a judgment as to the truth of those words. When we throw a ball in the air, it will fall to the earth without an outside force acting upon it. Those words are true because they mirror the reality of what we call gravity. God designed the world with predictable physical laws. From the observation of these laws, we design and build a myriad of machines and devices to benefit our lives. They work because the laws are true and fixed. In the same way, because we are created by God, there are laws that govern us emotionally, spiritually, and socially. God has given us the precepts and principles in his Word by which we can live happily and peacefully based upon the reality of who we are. If we accept that and follow those principles, we will experience the promised blessings. Through the prophet Malachi, God was rebuking the people of Israel for failing to follow his law and bring their tithes to him. In imploring the people to repent and follow his command, God said, "And try me now in this."[1] He asked the people to test his Word and follow it, and the blessings would come. In the same way today, when we follow the principles God has laid before us in his Word for ordering our society, they will work, for they are truth. Throughout the centuries, God's Word has always proven itself true. In science, history, sociology, and every subject the Bible speaks of, it has mirrored reality.

This doesn't mean there will be a perfect society ruled by men. We have already discussed there will never be a perfect society, a utopia, until Jesus Christ sets up his eternal kingdom. But until then, God has given us instructions for how society is to be governed. It is a plan that gives all men the best possible opportunity in this sin-cursed world.

Because of sin, we will always live in an imperfect place until Christ's kingdom. There will still be the reality of unwanted things. I spoke of this in relationship to the limits of what the government can do, and there is a reality of unwanted things in our individual lives as well. In this world there will always be evil, hatred, crime, sickness, poverty, war, drought, famine, and death. That is a consequence of man's sin. There is no man or government that can change that; only Jesus Christ will change it. But God's design for society limits the effects of the unwanted things and provides comfort for those who suffer in them. It is the society we have spoken of where men are accountable to God for the use of their talents and gifts, and where the tremendous potential of the individual can be reached. It is the potential and gifts of the individual used before God that provide the basis for a strong economy that creates and provides for the needs of society.

God has established three spheres of responsibility by which society is to be governed: the home, the church, and government. When each of these operates within the sphere of authority and responsibility assigned to them, and alongside the other two, society will be at its best. When one or the other steps outside the limits assigned to them, society suffers.

God's Design:
The Home

God's design for a peaceful and ordered society begins with the fundamental unit of society, the family. The family is the first institution found in the Bible. It should be the first authority children encounter. It is the authority given the responsibility to take children and prepare them to be adults. It is the unit of society that is to be self-sufficient, working together to provide for the needs it has and taking care of those members who are suffering. We will discuss some of these responsibilities briefly. Volumes of books have been written on the family, and it is not our purpose to encompass all the aspects of family life. We want to look at the home and family in relationship to its role in society.

A home and family starts with marriage. God designed marriage as a beautiful illustration of his love for us, and a reflection of his image to the world. "So God created man in His own image; in the image of God He created him; male and female He created them" (Genesis 1:27).

Both man and woman were and are created in the image of God. Both can reflect his image to those around them. Man and woman were created for each other and working together in marriage, they give a more complete picture of the image of God. That is part of the meaning of the two becoming one flesh in marriage. The differences between men and women are to complement each other. From this union of man and woman, children are produced, and our existence continues. The union of man and woman as we have described it is marriage. That is truth, and it does correspond to the reality we see around us. All of nature reflects this truth. All the animal kingdom is male and female continuing their species together. The union of man and woman as the start of a family is a common thread throughout cultures around the world for all of history. It is dangerous to let this truth slip away.

In the modern effort to "redefine" marriage, we run the risk of losing an institution that is one of the three that God has given to have an ordered society. How? The answer goes back to the nature of truth. A thing is true because it exists. It is not possible to "redefine" marriage. There is by "nature's law" a union of man and woman that forms the core of family. We have always called that marriage. We cannot make that unique union disappear. If we change the word *marriage* to include other things, that unique union will still exist by nature's law. But now we have nothing to call it. The word *marriage* will no longer have a unique definition. It can be whatever anyone wants it to be. When we don't have a word to identify the unique union of nature created by God to reflect His image and continue our existence, its worth, place, reality, and significance in society will disappear. And we will lose all the benefits of the structure and order the family should bring to society. Oh, the law of the unique union will still exist; it is part of nature and cannot be destroyed. But like an undiscovered cure for a disease, it won't bring any benefit.

That is why we said earlier that when words lose their meaning, everything loses meaning, and we find ourselves in a culture without any meaning or values. Words are what we use to describe the reality of the things we see and experience in the world. To take that value away from words leaves us without anything that is fixed and tied to something that we can say is true. Is it any wonder culture seems to be adrift in confusion? We have hidden the moorings of truth by obfuscation. We cannot lose the truth of marriage and family.

The family is a microsociety, and it is here where we learn to take our place in the larger society of our community, nation, and world. Usually, a family consists of members of different ages and children of different genders who must learn to live in peace with each other and learn to live under the rules of the house. Each individual needs skills to succeed in society. God has entrusted the care and instruction of children to the parents. Throughout the Old Testament, children were to be subject to parents, and parents had the responsibility and authority to direct in their children's lives. They were also commanded to teach and train them to be productive adults. Deuteronomy 6:7 says, "You shall teach them diligently to your children, and shall talk of them when you sit in your house, when you walk by the way, when you lie down, and when you rise up." And in Proverbs 22:6, we read, "Train up a child in the way he should go, and when he is old he will not depart from it." This ideal is repeated in the New Testament in such places as Ephesians 6:1–4: "Children, obey your parents in the Lord, for this is right…And you, fathers, do not provoke your children to wrath, but bring them up in the training and admonition of the Lord."

Again we see how God's Word corresponds to the reality of the world around us. The family with children is a basic unit of cultures around the world, and in the animal kingdom we see the young raised and taught by at least one, but at times both parents, to be adults within the species. An observation of the structure and order in the world around us reveals to us things about the nature and character of God. Romans 1:19–20 states,

> Because what may be known of God is manifest in them, for God has shown it to them. For since the creation of the world His invisible attributes are clearly seen, being understood by the things that are made, even His eternal power and Godhead, so that they are without excuse.

God's creation is a witness to all mankind of who God is and the truth that he has established. This truth has been called the "law of nature" by the great legal scholar, Sir William Blackstone.[1] There is a great statement in the Declaration of Independence that further expounds on this ideal and lays down this principle as a foundation for our nation. The writers appealed to this authority for independence "to assume among the Powers of the earth, the separate and equal station to which the Laws of Nature and of Nature's God entitle them…we hold these truths to be self-evident."[2] The truths referred to are those revealed in nature that are self-evident by observation. And so it is with the family as the basic unit of society

It is important to note that although the Scripture references we have cited instruct parents to bring up and train their children about the God of Israel and Christianity, that is not a condition of parental authority. God does not compel anyone to worship him. He instructs us in the truth, leaves a witness for man in creation, and fully revealed himself in the person of Jesus Christ. But the choice to believe is up to man. Likewise, parental authority is only restricted when the life and health of the child is in danger. Parents are accountable to God for how and what they teach their children. Parental authority must be defended.

Although not always the case, generally no one will care about the nurturing and instruction of children like the parents will. If the family is elevated again to its lofty place in society, that care would only flourish. It wasn't until the traditional values of family were targeted and denigrated in the beginning of the 1960s and the government intervened and took away the role of the father as provider through entitlement programs that the family unit began to crumble. Oh, there were always broken homes, but the percentages have increased so drastically that today, an intact family unit with biological parents is the oddity. That is why it is so important that the natural unique units of society retain their identity through the words we use. Marriage should identify a unique and looked up to institution; family should mean a home with mother and father, and those homes that are broken up should be the minority to maintain a healthy society.

When a nation is made up of healthy families, it has a myriad of little microsocieties, where character and values are being taught, respect for authority is learned, the rights of siblings as individuals is seen, and individual needs are being met. The Bible is very clear that families are to provide for their own well-being. "But if anyone does not provide for his own, and especially for those of his household, he has denied the faith and is worse than an unbeliever" (1 Timothy 5:8). So it is in the family that the needs for food, shelter, clothing, help, aid, and nurturing are to be met. That is the directive and intent of God for the family. All that is needed to sustain life is to be provided for within the family unit. If we step back and look at the list of needs we just mentioned and compare them to the needs of an individual we might see out on the street, we see they fall within the category of what the family should provide. For an individual to be well and healthy, they need food, clothing, and shelter. From there, we would say they need love and companionship. Next, they would need help and encouragement to develop their gifts and talents so they could be independent and if they so chose, start a family of their own. All these needs can and should be provided within the family unit. It is the responsibility given to the family by God.

The family is the best place for the development of gifts and talents to begin to take place. Again, it starts in the marriage relationship. Men and women are created different, but equal before God. Each is specifically gifted and talented by God. And ideally, a marriage should be both a man and woman helping each other to be all that God created *each* to be, that together, they might be all God wants *them* to be. This nurturing and encouraging of gifts and talents should then naturally extend to children as well. Most parents by nature want to see their children excel. In God's design for society, where responsibility and accountability are placed on the individual, it is imperative that every person is encouraged to find their gifts and excel. That takes place best within the family.

Perhaps some are thinking this all sounds good, but that isn't the way life goes. Indeed, the reality of unwanted things encroaches upon the family unit as well; divorce, abandonment, neglect, and abuse are all part of some families. At times the self-interest of man in our fallen human nature is so great that people destroy their own families to fulfill their own selfish desires. But just because something is difficult doesn't mean we should abandon the goal. These ideals of family need to be lifted up, taught and respected, like a beautiful picture that people want to get closer to so they can see it more clearly. Attempting to change words, meanings, and the definitions of marriage and family hides the picture from view. And when there isn't a vision to follow, the ideal will never be reached.

How can we deny that abandoning an ideal doesn't change society's actions? There was a time when purity was lifted up as an ideal. Was it always followed? No. But, by lifting up the standard, people believed in something better, and some worked at achieving it. Just look at the changes in sexual behavior in the last fifty to sixty years. Once, it was shocking when two lived together without being married. Now, many don't even bother to marry, and some would be shocked if they were told they shouldn't live with their boyfriend or girlfriend, truly shocked that someone thought there was something wrong with it. It honestly never entered their mind. Why? Because, they had never been taught or exposed to a righteous ideal. Who would argue that the consequences of rampant immorality are beneficial to society? Our society is full of single-parent homes, homes with children from different mothers and fathers, and individuals weighted down with emotional, psychological, and spiritual damage from promiscuity. This is not an atmosphere that produces the love, care, and support that is needed for children and individuals to flourish. This is not a condemnation of people affected in the ways described, but a condemnation that we as a society have failed to hold up standards for people to strive for. Life is filled with the reality of unwanted things. When divorce and abandonment happen, our response should be to reach out in love to help and support those in need. And God is always gracious to forgive and bless. I know wonderful, loving couples and children from blended families. Society and families will never be perfect, but we should never abandon the picture of the ideal. Our twenty-sixth president, Theodore Roosevelt, stated about disregarding marriage "that such disregard if at all common means the complete moral disintegration of the body politic."[3] Standards in a society do not change because God has changed his mind; they change because man follows his own mind. Ideals, or the lack of them, will change culture.

The family is the first and foremost unit of society. In fact, the family was designed and intended by God to be so complete that the other two institutions would not be necessary if it were not for sin. That concept gives us a better picture of the role of the other two institutions in society.

GOD'S DESIGN: THE CHURCH

The next institution God has given in his design for an ordered society is the church. (The order of home, church, and government are not given here chronologically as they are revealed in Scripture, but given in order of proximity to the family unit which is first chronologically.) To those reading this who are not Christian and to whom the word *church* brings disgust or bad memories (perhaps rightly so), you may look at church as charity, as it fits in society. I am not saying they are analogous, but making an allowance so that the argument may be followed to its conclusion. My harshest criticism for the condition of our society, the expanded role of the federal government, and for the one institution that has failed the most in fulfilling the role given to it by God, is the church. Organized religion has committed unspeakable atrocities through the centuries in the name of Christ. But true Christianity has blessed this country and the world with love, care, the hope of forgiveness through Jesus Christ, and an outstretched hand to the needy. In the last century, those of us who profess Christianity have abandoned the principles of God's Word, walked away from faith in God for our needs, and abdicated our role in society to the government for the sake of security and our own slothfulness. This is not to condemn all Christians. Many individuals and local churches have worked faithfully and tirelessly to do what is right and to be faithful to the church's role in society. But taken as a whole, for those who take the name of Christ, we have failed. We have already spoken that it is natural for those who are not Christian to seek the security we all crave from the government, but it is shameful for Christians to do so.

In speaking of the church, we are not speaking of any one denomination, but the church being made up of every follower of Jesus Christ throughout the world. It is through the local organized groups of believers that the work of the church is carried out. The church is different from the other two institutions God has given for an ordered society in that the church does not have authority within society. There is an ecclesiastical authority within the church that each denomination and group defines in various ways, but God has not given the church authority over society. We have already seen that the family is given authority over the care and upbringing of children and the responsibility to provide for their own needs. The government is given authority within society as well, but that is not the role of the church. Israel, in the Old Testament, was a theocracy, a type of the future kingdom under Christ; that failed and it was designed to show the failure of men's sinful hearts. Jesus made it very clear that now, the church is not to be a theocracy. In John 18:36, Jesus said, "My kingdom is not of this world. If My kingdom were of this world, My servants would fight, so that I should not be delivered to the Jews, but now My kingdom is not from here." Also, in Acts before Jesus's ascension, the disciples were asking if Jesus would set up his kingdom. His response again gives us instruction about the church's mission.

> It is not for you to know times or seasons which the Father has put in His own authority. But you shall receive power when the Holy Spirit has come upon you; and you shall be witnesses to Me in Jerusalem, and in all Judea and Samaria, and to the end of the earth.[1]

Throughout this book as we have made arguments for what the government should not be doing and what the family should be doing, many have probably been screaming, "What happens when people don't take responsibility for themselves or need help?" That is the role God has given to the church. We have spoken of the reality of unwanted things, both as they relate to a nation, families, and individuals. Bad things happen to people who are making every effort to take care of themselves, or people will be irresponsible and suffer failure. There will always be needs within a society. Jesus said, "For the poor you have with you always." (John 12:8) A part of the role God has given to the church within society is to meet the needs of the suffering. We have listed the needs that should be met within the family: food, clothing, shelter, love, companionship, encouragement, and instruction. The church should act as an extended family to assist people in these needs and bring them to a place of supporting themselves. Along with this, the church is to give the good news of forgiveness through faith in Jesus Christ to lift up all who are burdened with sin, and the church should stand for and proclaim righteousness. This help, aid, and offer of forgiveness are open to all and not exclusive to those who believe. Faith is not a requirement to receive compassion. Historically, the church has started many of the institutions of higher learning in our nation. Hospitals, orphanages, nursing facilities, shelters, and prison ministries have all been started by the church. Many of these continue today. This is the church following in the example of Jesus, the early church, and the commands to us as believers today.

The Gospels give an account of the ministry of Jesus Christ upon the earth. When Peter was speaking to Cornelius in Acts 10:38, he gave this description of Jesus ministry: "How God anointed Jesus of Nazareth with the Holy Spirit and with power, who went about doing good and healing all who were oppressed by the devil, for God was with Him." Jesus "went about doing good." Was that the primary purpose for Jesus, God the Son, coming to earth? No. Jesus came to take the punishment for and die for our sin. Yet, in his ministry of telling the people to repent and believe in him as the fulfillment of God's promises in the Old Testament, he met the physical and spiritual needs of the people to demonstrate his power and love. It is the same for the church today. We are to show

God's love to the world through our actions in meeting the needs of the helpless. We then have an opportunity to speak of the spiritual needs of man.

The early church followed in the example of Jesus. We have already discussed the example of the early church selling their possessions to meet the needs of fellow believers. In addition to this, the apostles, given special gifts of healing as a witness to Jesus Christ, healed the sick. When Paul was saying farewell to the elders of the church in Ephesus, he reminded them of his example that they were to follow.

> I have coveted no one's silver or gold or apparel. Yes, you yourselves know that these hands have provided for my necessities, and for those who were with me. I have shown you in every way, by laboring like this, that you must support the weak. And remember the words of the Lord Jesus, that He said, 'It is more blessed to give than to receive.'[2]

Paul was a tentmaker by trade. There were those who supported Paul in his missionary journeys, but he also worked to support himself and have resources to give as well. Paul labored tirelessly to preach the gospel, but he didn't use that as an excuse not to work. Notice again the phrase "By laboring like this, that you *must* support the weak." Christians should be the hardest workers and the best in their fields of study and occupation. God is perfect, and as we represent Christ to the world, we should strive to be the best at all we do and set an example. But we also give labor our best effort so we can have extra to give to others in need.

The church today needs to continue in the example of Jesus and the early church. We do not go around healing and doing miracles. Oh, God still does miracles; the greatest, changing my selfish nature into a nature of love and care for others. Every believer is the miracle the world should see, and they see it through acts of kindness and compassion. And God still can heal the sick. But the miracles and signs were for the early apostles to begin the spread of Christianity. Paul left us with instructions too. "Therefore, as we have opportunity, let us do good to all, especially to those who are of the household of faith" (Galatians 6:10). The church does good by being that extended family to all men, building hospitals and schools, and giving help to those met with disaster.

Many people today are familiar with the Salvation Army as a charitable organization that provides disaster assistance and help to those suffering misfortune. This organization was started by one couple fulfilling the instructions of Scripture we have looked at. In 1865, William Booth was preaching to the poor and outcasts of society on London's East Side. The success of his ministry in converting people to Christianity and his desire to meet the needs of the new believers both spiritually and physically led to the founding of what became known in 1878 as the Salvation Army. Today the Salvation Army provides a myriad of programs to assist people, from disaster assistance to prison ministries and rehabilitation services around the world. This phrase still remains in their mission statement: "Its mission is to preach the gospel of Jesus Christ and to meet human needs in His name without discrimination."[3] What a wonderful statement of what the church today should be doing.

One of my favorite verses is James 1:27. "Pure and undefiled religion before God and the Father is this: to visit orphans and widows in their trouble, and to keep oneself unspotted from the world." What does God want from us as believers? That we should be holy and righteous in our personal lives and take care of the helpless. Have we done this? Why in America, with the wealth we have and the number of professing Christians there are, is there one orphan child not adopted in this country? Why have Christians abandoned dependence on God and one another for promises of security from the government? Why has the church abdicated its God-given role to be the safety net for society? The answer is in our own sinful hearts. It's too easy to let the government take the place the church is to occupy. For believers, the first step to restoring a society based on God's design is our own repentance for our culpability.

GOD'S DESIGN: GOVERNMENT

Government is not charity. We have spent time discussing the need for government and its God-given purpose as an institution, to punish evil. We have discussed the limits of what government can do because it is a human organization limited by the ability of man. And we have looked at the founders' vision for a government that was limited to specific delegated powers. As we discussed the expansion of the federal government, we pointed to the desire of men to have security and seek that security from the government. Another reason for the expansion of the federal government is the mistaken view that the role of government is to act as the church or a charity.

Earlier we spoke of the good intentions of some of the early progressives. In 1911, Woodrow Wilson stated, "America was born a Christian nation, America was born to exemplify that devotion to the elements of righteousness which are derived from the revelations of Holy Scripture."[1] That is a statement that I wholeheartedly agree with, if we are speaking of America as its individual citizens reflecting Christian character and its institutions following their roles "derived from the revelations of Holy Scripture." I do not doubt President Wilson's faith, devotion to God, or his desire to make America a better nation. But the government can only "exemplify righteousness" by acting within the boundaries set by God. What President Wilson and other progressives did is personify the government and try to make it act like the church, family, or an individual. Oddly, that is the very thing Liberals today claim Conservatives want to do. In 1976, Jimmy Carter stated, "We have a responsibility to try to shape government so that it does exemplify the will of God."[2] Again, I do not question President Carter's faith or sincerity. But I believe both Presidents Wilson and Carter failed to see God's design for the government in an ordered society given within the Scriptures, and that only God's design will bring the best hope for a peaceful and productive society based on human nature.

The government cannot be charitable. The government is not a person. By definition, charity speaks of a voluntary action based on good will. The government is an instrument of force by its biblical definition, and by its empirical existence. When a government attempts charity, it forcefully takes from one individual and gives it to another. That is not charity. God does not violate the human will. That is the basis for freedom. We are individuals before God, accountable to him for our actions. Mankind is God's property. Revelation 4:11 states, "For You created all things, and by Your will they exist and were created." And Romans 9:21, in speaking of God's sovereignty, states,

"Does not the potter have power over the clay..." The potter and clay are an analogy of mankind in God's hand. God has given us our lives, gifts, and talents, and placed us in an environment with resources, all to use and be accountable to him. That is the basis for individual rights. Our life, what we own, and the decisions we make about sustaining our life are things that ultimately belong to God. No individual, group, or government should violate those things. The government's role is to protect those rights and freedoms and intervene when men take away the rights of another. For the government to step in and violate human will by forcing "charity" is a perversion of God's design for society. It is the government stepping in and becoming the entity taking away the rights of men. Sadly, as we have already spoken, too many in the church and society see the government as fulfilling the mission of the church or charity. That is an easy excuse for people to do nothing.

As we look at God's design for government, we see it is largely defined by the two institutions we have already discussed: the home and the church. The desire of men is to live in a peaceful society where our needs are met. As we have discussed the things that are needed for that to be possible, we have seen that God assigned the provision for physical needs and instruction to live in society to the family. To the church, God has assigned the responsibility to teach righteousness, faith, love, and care for those in need. What is yet needed? As explained earlier, because we live in a world where evil exits, and we are all guilty to varying degrees of that evil, an institution is needed to restrain and punish evil. That is the role God has assigned to governments. 1 Peter 2:13–14 states,

> Therefore submit yourselves to every ordinance of man for the Lord's sake, whether to the king as supreme, or to governors, as to those who are sent by him for the punishment of evildoers and for the praise of those who do good.

We will repeat part of Romans 13:4 again here. "But if you do evil, be afraid; for he does not bear the sword in vain; for he is God's minister, an avenger to execute wrath on him who practices evil." In part, evil is defined as taking away or encroaching upon the rights of another. Thus, the Declaration of Independence states, "That to secure these rights, Governments are instituted among men." This is the role of government and the basis for which it is established. What does that look like on a practical level? In what areas does the government have legitimate biblical authority?

The first area is the defense of the nation from attack by other nations. It is interesting that as men began to spread out upon the earth and settled in various regions, it seems God protected their right to exist in that place. It was only when the sin of a nation reached the point of demanding God's judgment that God removed a people from being a nation. A verse that illustrates this is Genesis 15:16. "But in the fourth generation they shall return here, for the iniquity of the Amorites is not yet complete." In context, God is telling Abraham what will be in the future and repeating his promise to Abraham that God would give his descendents the land of Canaan. But there would be a delay in possessing the land because God in his mercy was not yet ready to cast out the Amorites for their sin. Throughout history, nations have been overrun and occupied, but in time most have returned to their historical ethnic regions. In recent history, we have seen this take place in the former Soviet Union. With the breakup of the Union, independent and autonomous nations have again sprung up in traditional ethnic areas. Outside forces that would invade our nation put our life, property, rights, and freedom at risk. It is the government's legitimate, God-given role to protect our rights from such attacks. Another unwanted reality of the world in which we live is that the world is ruled by force. We cannot change that. The strong use force to overrun the weak. Without a strong national defense, our nation would be overrun by those who do not value individual rights and freedom. As long as America recognizes the rights of all people across the globe and values freedom, the best assurance of peace is a strong American military. Our nation has shed its blood repeatedly for the liberation of oppressed people. We cannot give others freedom for freedom must be taken up by each man. But we can and have liberated people to be able to choose freedom.

The government is also given the role of punishing evil. To emphasize Romans 13:4 again, the government is "an avenger to execute wrath on him who practices evil." It is not the role of government to reform criminal offenders. That is a role God has given to the church to preach the gospel of Christ that alone can change our evil hearts. The government's role is to punish. And punishment is a deterrent to crime. Ecclesiastes 8:11 instructs us, "Because the sentence against an evil work is not executed speedily, therefore the heart of the sons of men is fully set in them to do evil." Again, this is a truth that corresponds to reality. When we are traveling and see a law enforcement vehicle on the highway, our first instinct is to slow down and look at the speedometer. The presence of an officer and the thought of consequences results in a change of behavior. Crime in states that pass concealed carry laws generally goes down. The threat of an armed potential victim is a deterrent to criminals. The government's role is to punish in a timely manner. God instituted safeguards for justice within the nation of Israel by never allowing the death penalty without two witnesses to convict of guilt (Numbers 35:30). Our justice system has many safeguards to try and ensure that the truth is determined and justice is truly served. This is right and will take some time. If the government stays within the role designed by God, there will be enough resources to be sure the process moves at a steady pace. Diverting resources of government to other places strains and slows the justice system.

As individuals, we have a right to self defense. This is expressed biblically and implied by natural law in our right to life. But, individuals do not have a right to punish evil doers, nor do individuals have a right to take another life outside of defense or when acting under the legitimate authority of the government. Perhaps the tendency to personify government has led some to question or hesitate at the government's role to punish. But if the government is viewed as an institution specifically given by God for this purpose, there isn't a conflict between the commands in Scripture for man's relationship to his fellow man ("You shall not murder" Exodus 20:13) and government actions involving the punishment of wrongdoing. Government should not infringe upon the rights of an innocent individual, but criminal actions forfeit certain individual rights, at times even the right to life. The Bible instructs the government to carry out capital punishment in several places, including Numbers 35 where God warns the nation of Israel not to be slack in carrying out the death penalty. Verse 33 states, "So you shall not pollute the land where you are; for blood defiles the land, and no atonement can be made for the land, for the blood that is shed on it, except by the blood of him who shed it." This is implied again in Romans 13:4: "For he does not bear the sword in vain." The sword was an instrument to bring death, and the instructions for the government throughout the New Testament do not remove the obligation to carry out the death penalty for murder cases.

To have a correct understanding of God's design for society it is so important that we see the roles God ordained for each institution. We cannot attempt to make an individual act according to the commands for the government, and we cannot attempt to make a government act according to the commands for individuals. Every institution of God has its proper place and its own rules. When we begin to confuse the instructions for individual behavior with those for the home or church or government, we lose sight of the purpose for each. And in effect we are trying to "force a square peg through a round hole." It won't work. The institution won't be able to perform its role in society.

The government is also given the role of an arbiter in preserving the rights of men. It is important that we don't misunderstand what that means. The government is not the source or creator of rights; rights naturally exist to us as God's creation. Rights can be discussed, understood, and taught, but they are finite; they cannot be expanded or changed. The government is to use its authority to settle disputes based on natural rights. The laws of a nation should all be based upon some natural right and enforced to secure rights or punish the infringement of rights.

We see the Apostle Paul recognizing and using this role of government in Acts 25:9–11.

> But Festus, wanting to do the Jews a favor, answered Paul and said, 'Are you willing to go up to Jerusalem and there be judged before me concerning these things?' So Paul said, 'I stand at Caesar's judgment seat, where I ought to be judged. To the Jews I have done no wrong, as you very well know. For if I am an offender, or have committed anything deserving of death, I do not object to dying; but if there is nothing in these things of which these men accuse me, no one can deliver me to them. I appeal to Caesar.'

The context for these verses is the occasion of Paul being falsely accused by the Jewish leaders in Jerusalem for violating the temple by bringing in a gentile. Fearing his right to a just trial being denied at Jerusalem, Paul, a Roman citizen, used his privileges of citizenship to appeal to Caesar to be an arbitrator for his case.

The government acts in this role by ensuring that all men have equal opportunity to exercise their rights. We have already looked at one way the government does this when we discussed the Commerce Clause in the constitution. As stated previously, the Commerce Clause exists to ensure the free flow of goods and services between the states. This allows all men to trade and sell what they produce among several states. The basis for this law is the right to liberty. Equal opportunity does not mean equal outcomes or guaranteed success. Some are mistaken by thinking the government exists to guarantee the success of all. Success or failure is between God and the individual. The government's only role is to make sure no one takes away our right to try and succeed.

The government also acts in this role by settling disputes over issues such as water rights. Property rights don't extend to stopping the flow of water on a stream going through a person's property. The water is for all to use along the course of the stream. If a dispute arises over the use of water, government has a role to act as arbitrator. This same reasoning is a basis for pollution and environmental law. An individual cannot act upon their property in such a way that it destroys the property of another. But it is imperative for the government to use the minimum necessary regulation. Anything beyond this crosses a fine line that will encroach upon the individual's right to use the resources God has given him to be productive and sustain his life. Admittedly, these are not easy decisions, as they are comparative to walking on the edge of a knife. Leaders, judges, and officials with integrity and high esteem for natural rights are crucial to making wise decisions. Yet how can we expect such qualities from those in authority when many of the principles we have discussed have been abandoned, the concept of truth has become relative, and society simply does "what is right in their own eyes"?[3]

One final example of the government's proper use of this role of arbiter is to intervene anywhere the natural rights of men is abused. God has given authority over children to the family, but that authority cannot be used to injure or neglect a child. The government has an obligation to intervene and determine the best care for the child based on the rights of other families who may be willing to provide that care. God has allowed men to freely choose to worship him, or ignore him. This forms a basis for our right to freedom of religion. But no religious expression has the right to abuse or destroy life, liberty, or property. Here again, the government has an obligation to intervene and protect the rights of individuals. All these issues require great care in maintaining proper balance and respect for rights. But it must start with an understanding of the nature of rights.

The government fulfills a vital role in God's design for an ordered society. It is designed and instituted to manage the consequences of evil, and thus solve a problem. The government only becomes a problem when it steps outside the role given to it by God.

AN APPEAL TO HUMANITY

The writer of Ecclesiastes, upon coming to the end of his thoughts, wrote, "Let us hear the conclusion of the whole matter."[1] And so it would be well to conclude this argument for a limited government. Although I have spoken of government, my motivation for writing is not political. I do not take any pleasure in putting forth solutions to political problems simply for the sake of argument.

My motivation is the well-being of people. I am deeply saddened by what a government that has stepped outside its biblical role has done to the human spirit. The government has replaced God in the lives of many individuals. It is the entity that is looked at to provide security and all that is needed for life. That is God's role. I feel compelled to defend the honor of the God I love, who has first loved me. The God of Abraham, Isaac, and Jacob; the God of the nation of Israel; of whom Jesus Christ, God the Son, came in the flesh; has infinitely equipped and gifted each of us as individuals to live happy and fulfilled lives before him. My great desire is that each person might know the joy of using their God-given talents to work and be productive with the special skills they possess. God has given us three institutions that we might live in a peaceful society where our needs are met and the human potential can be encouraged. I'm sickened by the death, destruction, and poverty that man's attempts at ruling his way through strong central collective governments have brought about. We have spoken of the reality of unwanted things that will always be with us. But hopefully, we have also seen that even through these difficulties, God's love can be demonstrated, and our own lives can be enriched by acts of charity and love expressed for our fellow man.

God has also left us with the promise of a future kingdom when there will be no death, crying, or pain. He freely offers us a place in that kingdom on a new earth, free from all the difficulties of this life, when our true God-given potential will be revealed; a place where we will eternally experience the joy of using our talents to be productive, with family, friends, love, and good will for all men. We will forever experience the security and love of our God who saved us.

All this he offers to us through Jesus Christ. God originally intended man to live in such a place. The world was first created a perfect place, but sin entered and that was lost. Because God is just and holy, the punishment for sin is death and separation from him. But God's love compelled him to satisfy his own demands for justice that we might be saved from the penalty we deserved. Jesus Christ, eternally God the Son, left heaven, came to earth and lived a sinless life of love and service to men and the Father. He willing offered up himself as a sacrifice for our sin on a Roman cross, so that we might be with him eternally. Having fully paid our penalty, he rose from the dead, proving he has the right and power to give us eternal life. This he offers to us. He simply says come. "Come to Me, all you who labor and are heavy laden, and I will give you rest" (Matthew 11:28). A thief, dying beside our Lord, conscious of his own guilt and just damnation, turned to Jesus in helplessness and said, "Lord, remember me when You come into Your kingdom." Our Lord's response was, "Assuredly, I say to you, today you will be with Me in paradise" (Luke 23:42–43). Those same words of assurance and peace are offered today to all who will come to Jesus like the thief—simply seeking forgiveness through him. I plead with everyone to accept his offer.

So we are left with choices before us. The choice of what we will do with our own sin. God has given us an offer. We also have a choice of what the future of our nation will look like. Will we look at the evidence of God's Word, of history, of the reality of failed government promises, and choose to order our society God's way? Many gave their lives to give us the chance to live free. To have liberty to use our gifts before God, to live lives filled with fruitful labor and love and joy. We stand at a place in history where that chance of freedom is slipping away. Now, we can still make a choice for freedom that will only cost us a little more work and effort. Once freedom is lost, a future generation will give their blood to try and get it back. These are our times; this is our choice.

I enjoy J.R.R. Tolkien's work *The Lord of the Rings* for the many life lessons he incorporates into the stories. As I reflect on our time and the choices that lay before us, I'm reminded of Frodo lamenting to Gandalf of Sauron's return to Mordor. "'I wish it need not have happened in my time,' said Frodo. 'So do I,' said Gandalf, 'and so do all who live to see such times. But that is not for them to decide. All we have to decide is what to do with the time that is given to us.'" [2]

Endnotes

The Need for Government

1   Ecclesiastes 1:10

2   C.S. Lewis, Mere Christianity, (New York: Harper Collins, 1952), 3-25.

3   Albert Hyma, and Mary Stanton, Streams of Civilization Volume One, (Arlington Heights: Christian Liberty Press, 1976), 37.

4   Ibid., 62-63.

Human Nature

1   Roman 3:23

2   Colossians 3:11

3   Psalm 139:13-16

The Utopian Failure

1   Sir Thomas More, Utopia, (Mineola: Dover Publications Inc, 1997), iii.

2   Karl Marx, and Fredereick Engels, Manifesto of The Communist Party in The Communist Manifesto: A Modern Edition, (New York: Verso, 1998).

3   Eric Hobsbawm, The Communist Manifesto: A Modern Edition, (New York: Verso, 1998), 3.

4   Leitenberg, Milton. Cornell University Peace Studies Program, Occasional Paper #29, "Deaths in Wars and Conflicts in the 20th Century." Last modified 2006. Accessed January 6, 2014. http://www.cissm.umd.edu/papers/files/deathswarsconflictsjune52006.pdf.,9

5   Ibid.

6   Ibid.

7   Ibid.

8   Ibid., 76.

9   Ibid., 11.

10 Ibid., 76.

11 Ibid., 77.

12 Commonly attributed to Lord Acton in a letter to Bishop Mandell Creighton in 1887.

Martin, Gary. The Phrase Finder, "Power corrupts; absolute power corrupts absolutely." Accessed January 6, 2014. http://www.phrases.org.uk/meanings/absolute-power-corrupts-absolutely.html.

13 Gunson, Phil. "Hugo Chavez Obituary." The Guardian, March 05, 2013. http://www.theguardian.com/world/2013/mar/05/hugo-chavez (accessed January 6, 2014).

14 Gye, Hugo, and Jill Reilly. "Was Chavez worth over $1bn when he died? Intelligence analyst claims he amassed huge fortune from country's oil wealth." Mail Online, March 07, 2013. http://www.dailymail.co.uk/news/article-2289427/Was-Hugo-Chavez-worth-1bn-died-Claims-amassed-huge-fortune-countrys-oil-wealth.html (accessed January 6, 2014).

Freedom

1 The American Heritage Dictionary of the English Language, New College Edition, (Boston: Houghton Mifflin Company, 1981).

2 Noah Webster, An American Dictionary of the English Language, (New York: S. Converse, 1828). Reprint by Rosalie Slater, (San Francisco: Foundation for American Christian Education, 1967).

3 ("American Heritage Dictionary of the English Language, New College Edition" 1981)

4 Judges 17:6

5 2 Thessolonians 3:10

6 Catherine Millard, Great American Statesmen and Heroes, (Camp Hill: Horizon Books, 1995), 130.

The Founder's Vision

1 "The Constitution of the United States" (1787) in The Federalist Papers, (New York: Bantam Books, 1982), 461-62.

2 Alexander Hamilton, James Madison, and John Jay, The Federalist Papers, (New York: Bantam Books, 1982), 213.

3 Albert Speer, Inside the Third Reich, (New York: Simon and Schuster, 1970), 221.

4 Ibid., 268.

5 ("Federalist Papers" 1982) 452.

6 "The Unanimous Declaration of the Thirteen United States of America" (1776) in Michael Farris, Constitutional Law, (Purcellville: Home School Legal Defense Association, 1998), 14.

7 Frederic Bastiat, The Law, (Irvington-on-Hudson: Foundation for Economic Education, 1998), 1.

8   Ibid., 7.

Private Property Rights

1   Matthew 20:1-15

2   Acts 5:1-10

Federal Expansion

1   The Heritage Foundation, "Charts on Federal Entitlement Spending as a Percentage of US Budget." Accessed January 8, 2014. http://www.heritage.org/federalbudget/budget-entitlement-programs.

2   Benson, Guy. "America's True National Debt: $87 Trillion." Townhall.com, November 28, 2012. http://townhall.com/tipsheet/guybenson/2012/11/28/americas_true_national_debt_87_trillion (accessed January 8, 2014).

3   ("Federalist Papers" 1982) 454.

4   Ibid., 463.

5   (Webster 1828)

Federal Expansion: The Commerce Clause

1   ("Federalist Papers" 1982) 455.

2   Ibid., 71-72.

3   Ibid., 213-214.

4   Michael Farris, Constitutional Law, (Purcellville: Home School Legal Defense Association, 1998), 84.

5   Ibid., 94.

6   Ibid

Federal Expansion: The Abandonment of Federalism

1   ("American Heritage Dictionary of the English Language, New College Edition" 1981)

2   ("Federalist Papers" 1982) 464.

3   Ibid., 152.

4   Ibid

5   Ibid., 194.

6   Roberts, Chief Justice. "NATIONAL FEDERATION OF INDEPENDENT BUSINESS ET AL.v SEBELIUS, SECRETARY OF HEALTH AND HUMAN SERVICES, ET AL." June 28, 2012. http://www.supremecourt.gov/opinions/11pdf/11-393c3a2.pdf (accessed January 8, 2014), 51-65.

7   ("Federalist Papers" 1982) 193.

8   Ibid., 313.

Federal Expansion: The Income Tax

1   ("Federalist Papers" 1982) 452.

2   Ibid., 456.

3   Ibid., 172

4   "Income Tax", The World Book Encyclopedia, 1956 ed.

5   ("Federalist Papers" 1982) 467.

6   Richard Lee, The American Patriots Bible, (Nashville: Thomas Nelson, 2009), 1323.

7   ("Federalist Papers" 1982) 168-169.

8   Ibid., 172.

9   Ibid., 102.

God's Design for an Ordered Society

1   Malachi 3:10

God's Design: The Home

1   (Lee 2009) 1280.

2   "The Unanimous Declaration of the Thirteen United States of America" (1776) in (Farris 1998) 14.

3   (Lee 2009) 1421.

God's Design: The Church

1   Acts 1:7-8

2   Acts 20:33-35

3   The Salvation Army, "Doing the Most Good." Accessed January 9, 2014. http://salvationarmyusa.org/usn/mission-statement.

God's Design: Government

1   (Lee 2009) 1278.

2   Ibid

3   Judges 17:6

An Appeal to Humanity

1   Ecclesiastes 12:13

2   J.R.R. Tolkien, The Lord of the Rings, The Fellowship of the Ring, (New York: Ballantine Books, 1954), 55-56. php?reqstyleid=10&mode=form&rsid=1&reqsrcid=Chicago-Book&more=yes&nameCnt=1.

CPSIA information can be obtained
at www.ICGtesting.com
Printed in the USA
LVHW052131301222
736235LV00034B/1279